THE
LOST
PROSPERITY
SECRETS
OF
NAPOLEON HILL

THE
LOST
PROSPERITY
SECRETS
OF
NAPOLEON HILL

Newly Discovered Advice
for Success in Tough Times
from the Renowned Author of
Think and Grow Rich

MEDIA

Published 2019 by Gildan Media LLC
aka G&D Media
www.GandDmedia.com

Front Cover design by David Rheinhardt of Pyrographx

Interior design by Meghan Day Healey of Story Horse, LLC

Library of Congress Cataloging-in-Publication Data is available upon request

ISBN: 978-1-7225-0225-6

10   9   8   7   6   5   4   3   2   1

Contents

Editor's Preface

He was five-foot-six and his name was Napoleon Hill. Said by many to be the inventor of motivational writing, Napoleon is most certainly the guru of all success gurus, the author of the number one motivational seller of all time, *Think and Grow Rich*. Hill emerged from decidedly unforgiving circumstances, as did so many of his subjects, and he set out early to find the answer to the ever-fresh question: What makes a winner? He found, among other things, that a youth of poverty was more a guarantee of success than a golden childhood. It was to be only one of many surprises.

With a letter of introduction from Andrew Carnegie, Hill lured their secrets from the world's winners by doing what no one had thought to do before: He simply asked the greatest how they became great. In the process, against all odds, he became a winner himself, ultimately finding himself listed as a peer with Marcus Aurelius, Ralph Waldo Emerson and Ben Franklin.

But before he became *the* Napoleon Hill, he fulfilled a childhood dream by starting two magazines. He had "analyzed" half of the 25,000 people he would eventually mine for information by that time, so he was already well versed in wisdom. But the little man with the huge spirit was still in his thirties, and magazine journalism isn't book writing, after all, so Napoleon took advantage of the candor and personal revelations periodicals allow.

His books edify, but it's in his magazines that Napoleon Hill lets his hair down.

"Twenty-five of my thirty-six years were unhappy ones," is one of his revelations. But "nothing I have ever undertaken . . . has proved as successful or brought me as much real happiness as my work on this little magazine has done."

And it's in the comfort of his own magazine that Napoleon Hill feels safe enough to tell on himself: "The first time the notion ever struck me to own and edit a magazine, some fifteen years ago, my idea was to jump on everything that was bad and pick to pieces all that I did not like. The gods of fate must have intervened to keep me from starting such an enterprise at that time . . ."

More than one chapter in this book is devoted to Hill's reverence for what the shortsighted call "failure." His own life was such a series of victorious failures that, when in his fifties, he marveled that an entire decade had gone by without his having to face a personal disaster. But Napoleon Hill, often down but never out, never wavered from his "definite chief aim." He was to teach millions around the world that even luck can be changed and failures put to good use. How else would he have known that so securely, but at first hand?

"Success requires no explanation. Failure permits no alibis," he would later say with the authority only experience can offer.

Hill was born in 1883 in a one-room cabin in the hills of aptly named Wise County, Virginia. A wild, gun-toting, untamed child, he began his writing career at age thirteen as a "mountain reporter" for small town newspapers, and never lost his hunger for real facts about real people who overcame odds, including himself. It was this childhood job that taught him how to interview intimidating leaders about their losses and victories.

Napoleon Hill's is one of those it-seemed-to-be-bad-but-it-turned-out-good stories. His mother died when he was very young, but the educated, audacious woman his father then married was impatient with poverty, as Hill later put it. Hill's stepmother took responsibility for the family store and farm, sent his father to dental school at the age of 40 and gave Napoleon the backbone he needed to climb out of his Virginia valley. She placed in his mind the thought he would someday become most famous for: "What the mind of man can conceive, he can achieve."

These early writings of Napoleon Hill's, rarely seen before this, are refreshing and revealing. With his magazines as incubators, his own pages became testing grounds and launch pads for one of the most uplifting books of all time.

Patricia G. Horan

ONE

Learn How to Use That Wonderful Mind of Yours

The human mind is a composite of many qualities and tendencies. It consists of likes and dislikes, optimism and pessimism, hatred and love, constructiveness and destructiveness, kindness and cruelty. The mind is made up of all these qualities and more. It is a blending of them all, some minds showing one of these qualities dominating and other minds showing others dominating.

The dominating qualities are largely determined by one's environment, training, associates, and particularly by one's own thoughts! Any thought held constantly in the mind, or any thought dwelt upon through concentration and brought into the conscious mind, often attracts to it those qualities of the human mind that it most resembles.

A thought is like a seed planted in the ground, in that it brings back a crop after its kind, multiplies, and grows; therefore, it is dangerous to allow the mind to hold any thought that is destructive. Such thoughts must sooner or later seek release through physical action.

Through the principle of auto-suggestion—that is, thoughts held in the mind and concentrated upon—any thought will soon begin to crystallize into action. We will discuss this principle at length later.

If the principle of auto-suggestion were generally understood and taught in the public schools, it would change the whole moral and economic standards of the world inside of twenty years. Through this principle, the human mind can rid itself of its destructive tendencies by constantly dwelling upon its constructive tendencies such as positive thinking or a positive attitude. The qualities of the human mind need the sunlight of nourishment and use to keep them alive. Throughout the universe, there is a law of nourishment and use that applies to everything that lives and grows. This law has decreed that every living thing that is neither nourished nor used must die, and this applies to the qualities of the human mind we have mentioned.

The only way to develop any quality of the mind is to concentrate upon it, think about it, and use it. Evil tendencies of the mind can be blotted out by starving them to death through disuse!

What would it be worth to the young, plastic mind of the child to understand this principle and commence to make use of it early in life, beginning with kindergarten?

The principle of auto-suggestion is one of the fundamental major laws of applied psychology. Through a proper understanding of this principle the whole tendency of the human mind can be directed toward constructive effort in a short period of time.

Instead of merely waiting for someone to start a movement for general education along this line, why don't you begin now to make use of this principle for the benefit of you and yours? Your children may not be fortunate enough to receive this training in school, but there is nothing to hinder you from giving it to them in your home. There is nothing to hinder you from studying, understanding, and applying to your own efforts this principle from now on.

Learn something about that wonderful machine we call the human mind. It is your real source of power. If you are ever to free yourself of petty worries and financial want, it will be through the efforts of that wonderful mind of yours. This writer is still a young man, yet he has positive evidence of the transformation of both men and women from failure to success in remarkably short periods of time, ranging all the way from a few hours to a few months.

The book you hold in your hands is concrete evidence of the soundness of the argument that individuals can control their economic destiny, because these writings are a success built out of fifteen years of failure! You too can turn your past failure into success if you will understand and intelligently apply the principles of applied psychology. You can get to wherever you wish to go in life. You can find happiness instantly, once you master this principle, and you can build financial success as rapidly as you comply with the established practices and principles of economics.

There is nothing occult in thinking this way about the human mind., which functions in harmony with the physical and economic laws and principles. You do not need the assistance of any person on earth in the manipulation of your own mind so it will function as you want it to. Your mind is something that you control, no matter what your station in life may be, provided always that you exercise that right, instead of permitting others to do so for you.

Learn something of the powers of your mind! It will free you of the curse of fear and fill you with inspiration and courage.

HOW ANDREW CARNEGIE USED OTHER PEOPLE'S BRAINS

Andrew Carnegie passed away leaving a huge fortune after having given away another fortune.

There were thousands of people who envied his titanic wealth, and there were also many thousands of people who puzzled their brains trying to think out some plan or scheme through which they could build up a fortune such as the one Carnegie possessed.

Let us tell you how Carnegie built his fortune. Maybe it will give you an idea that will help you in building yours. In the first place, it is well to remember that Carnegie was not possessed of more ability than the average man enjoys. He was not a genius, and he did nothing that almost any other person could not duplicate.

Mr. Carnegie accumulated his millions by selecting, combining, and managing other people's brains. He realized early in life that any undertaking such as the steel business required more talent than any one person possessed. He also realized that most industries and businesses require at least two types of people—one the caretaker and the other the promoter. Carnegie selected the people he wanted, organized them, directed them, and kept them enthusiastic and eager to render the greatest amount of service. He got them to cooperate with one another and with him.

No one can build a fortune such as that which Carnegie controlled without the use of other people's brains. The amount a single brain can produce, accumulate, and own, acting independently of other brains, is comparatively little, but the amount one brain can accumulate and control when acting in harmony with other highly organized minds is practically unlimited.

If you want to become wealthy, learn how to attract men and women who have what you do not possess in the way of brain capacity. If you are of the promoter type, select your associates so that some of them will be of the caretaker type. A well-rounded-out partnership or organization, to be successful, must be made up of people who possess all the requisite qualities essential for success. Some people can acquire but cannot conserve assets. Other people can conserve but cannot acquire. The two types, working in harmony, can both acquire and conserve.

Many a business has grown sickly and finally passed into bankruptcy for no reason other than the fact that it was managed by people who had too much of one sort of talent and too little or none at all of other necessary sorts. Business requires something more than capital in order to succeed. It requires well-balanced brains, made up of the various shades and blending of the caretaker and the promoter types.

THE MAGICAL HUMAN MIND

This is no time for the person who believes only what he or she understands. Neither is it a favorable time for the person who doubts the ability of the human mind to look behind the curtain of time down the ages and there see the handwriting of nature. Nature is yielding up her secrets to all who wish to see. She no longer uses the lightning in the clouds to scare ignorant, superstitious humanity. That force has now been harnessed. It drives our wheels of industry and carries the whisper of our voices and even our fleeting thoughts around the earth in nanoseconds.

Electricity is exactly the same force now that it was hundreds of years ago, yet we knew nothing about it except that we believed it was only destructive! We did not know that it would one day serve as our greatest servant, obediently carrying out our commands. We did not understand electricity, so we made no attempt to master it until recent years. How can we discover the possibilities of the earth's natural forces?

We can do this only through experimentation—through the use of imagination! This is decidedly the age of imagination, inquiry, and experiment. The human race has begun to throw off the shackles of fear and doubt and take hold of the tools of progress that have been lying at our feet throughout the ages.

The present is the most wonderful age in the history of the human race—wonderful not only in its progressive inventions, but also in its mental development. Every day we announce to the world a new technology or invention, and none of it would be possible without the human mind.

WHY WE SHOULD QUIT QUARRELING WITH OUR NEIGHBORS

The time and energy we spend in striking back at those who anger us would make us independently wealthy, if this great force were directed toward constructive effort—to building instead of tearing down! The average person spends three-fourths of his or her lifetime in such useless, destructive effort.

There is but one real way to punish a person who has wronged you, and that is by returning good for evil. The hottest coals ever heaped upon a human being's head are acts of kindness offered in return for acts of cruelty. Time spent in hatred is not only wasted, but it smothers the only worthwhile emotions of the human heart, and renders a person useless for constructive work. Thoughts of hatred do not harm anyone except the person who indulges in them. Alcohol and drugs are no more deleterious to the human body than are thoughts of hatred and anger. Lucky is the person who has grown to be big enough and wise enough to rise above intolerance, selfishness, greed, and petty jealousies. These are the things that blot out the better impulses of the human soul and open the human heart to violence.

Anger never profited a person anything. Great souls are usually housed in human beings who are slow to anger and who seldom try to destroy their fellows or defeat them in their undertakings. The man or woman who can forgive and truly forget an injury is to be envied. Such souls rise to heights of happiness that most mortals never enjoy.

How long will it be until the human race will learn to walk down the pathway of life, arm in arm, helping one another in a spirit of love, instead of trying to cut one another down? How long will it be until we learn that the only real success in life is measured by the extent to which we serve humanity? How long will it be until we learn that life's richest blessings are bestowed upon the one who refuses to stoop to the vulgar attempt to destroy others?

TWO

Creating the Rich Vibration of Success

Most of us ask for success without the usual hardships that come with it. We want success with as little effort as possible. It is a good idea to define success in order to understand it, and write out a description of it as one of the items on our list of hoped-for achievements. I do not know what your definition of the term success is, but if I may impose my own definition on you, I would do so as follows:

Success is the sum total of one's acts and thoughts that have, on account of their positive, constructive nature, brought happiness and good cheer to the majority of one's associates in the past and those in the coming years.

You cannot possibly bring happiness, good cheer, and sunshine into the lives of those with whom you associate and not enjoy success yourself. Neither can you bring misery, despondency, and unhappiness to others and be a success.

If you cause other people to smile when you are near; if you carry with you that rich, vibrating, dynamic personality that causes people to be glad when you are near; if you speak and think of the beauties of life and persuade others to do the same; if you have eliminated cynicism, hatred, fear, and despondency from your own nature and filled their place with a wholesome love for all humanity, then you are bound to be a success!

Money is not evidence of success. It may be, in fact, evidence of failure, and will be if happiness and goodwill did not accompany it throughout the process through which it was accumulated. I value more highly than all the wealth in the world the pleasure—the thrilling joy—the happiness and contentment that has come to me as a result of the opportunity I have had during the past year to serve my fellows through my writings.

Could any amount of money buy such pleasure?

No! A thousand times, no! Pleasure comes from doing and not from acquiring! This is a lesson that some people seem never to learn, but it is a truth nevertheless. The roadway to that thing we call success leads only in one direction, and that is straight through the great field of human service. Any road that leads in other directions cannot possibly reach success.

I intend to try to be happier this year than I was last year, not by "acquiring" more worldly goods, although I could use these to advantage, but by serving more people through my writings and by bringing greater happiness to the members of my immediate family and my personal friends. If we cannot increase our measure of success in this manner, then we don't know how at all!

By no means do I recommend that anyone give up the pursuit of money as one means of finding success and happiness, but I strongly recommend that no one depend entirely upon the power of money for success.

I have never had enough money to cause me to quit trying to render service, but some whom I know have had, and the result was not what I call success.

THAT'S WHY FINANCIAL SUCCESS IS DANGEROUS

Financial success brings power, and power is a dangerous thing to those who have not learned how to use it justly and wisely. Great financial power has a decided tendency to promote intolerance and disregard for the rights of others. When you begin to succeed financially, you will need to watch your step more closely than ever before.

Financial success too often smothers the finer impulses of the human heart, and leads a person to the worship of the god of Mammon! It is the exception and not the rule when a person who accumulates great financial power without having tasted liberally of the dregs of poverty uses that power wisely. Real success cannot be measured in dollars. It is something that can be measured only by the quantity and the quality of service one renders for the good of others. If financial power takes away the desire to render useful service, then it may be properly interpreted as failure instead of success.

Watch your step as you begin to accumulate more money than you need for your daily use. Take care that it does not blind your eyes to the one sure pathway to real success, which is the performance of useful service for the good of humanity.

TWO MEN, TWO LEGS, BIG DIFFERENCE

In the town of Wichita Falls, Texas, I saw a one-legged man sitting on the sidewalk begging for a handout. A few questions brought out the fact that he had had a fair education. He said he was begging because no one would give him work. "The world is against me and I have lost confidence in myself," he said. Ah, there was the rub: "I have lost confidence in myself."

Across the hall from my office is another one-legged man. I have known him for several years and I know that his schooling was slight. He has less training than the one-legged beggar. But he is earning an impressive salary. as sales manager of a manufacturing concern, where he is directing a staff of fifty. The beggar displayed the stump of his amputated leg as evidence that he needs alms. The other one-legged man covered up the stump of his lost leg so it would not attract attention.

The difference between the two men exists merely in viewpoint. One believes in himself and the other does not. The one who believes in himself could give up the other leg and both of his arms and still earn a great deal of money. He could even give up both eyes, to boot, and still do very well.

The world never defeats you until you defeat yourself. A meat products manufacturer who was once at the top of his field became a wealthy man in the sausage business after paralysis had taken away the use of nearly every muscle in his body. He couldn't turn over in bed without aid. But he believed in himself, and as long as you have faith in yourself, and that wonderful mind of yours continues to function properly, you cannot be defeated in any legitimate undertaking. This statement is made without qualifications, because it is true.

THREE

16 Rungs On the Magic Ladder to Success

There is an indescribable "something" about *The Magic Ladder to Success* that attracts, holds, and inspires all who read it. It has helped thousands find their first step toward achievement. It appeals alike to the rich and the poor, the educated and the illiterate, and has the effect of bringing people together in a spirit of closer understanding.

The object of this Ladder is to show what human power is, and how it is developed in those who do not possess it. Human power comes only through organized knowledge intelligently directed. Facts within themselves do not represent power. Knowledge, unorganized and without intelligent control and direction, does not represent power.

There is a great deal of knowledge carefully classified and stored away on paper and electronically, but it represents no power until it is transformed into organized, intelligently directed effort. There is no power in college degrees, or in the education that these degrees represent, until it is classified, organized, and put into action. Instead, human power is organized and intelligently directed energy, as represented by facts, intelligence, and the faculties through which the human mind operates.

In weight, tensile strength and size, a strong chain in a sack full of disconnected chain links is impressive, but these links represent only a potential chain until they are organized, connected, and welded together. So it is with people's faculties. They must be organized before they represent power. There are two kinds of human power. One is represented by the organization of the individual faculties, which gives increased power to the individual, and the other is represented by the organization of individuals and groups of individuals.

A little handful of well-organized soldiers have been known to put to rout ten times its number of disorganized, undisciplined soldiers, and history is full of the biographies of people who have risen to fame and fortune through the process of organizing and intelligently directing their individual faculties, while millions around them, with equal opportunities, remained mediocre or out-and-out failures.

There is considerable energy in an ordinary small battery, but not enough to do bodily damage if someone should create a short circuit by touching it and absorb the entire charge. A thousand such batteries are equally harmless—until they are organized and connected together. Through this process of organization, if the energy of the entire thousand batteries is fed to one wire, enough energy is produced to turn a considerable piece of machinery. This group of batteries may be likened to individuals, in that greatly increased power comes through the organized effort of a large group of people, as compared to the efforts of the same people acting singly.

The object of this Ladder is mainly to direct attention to the modus operandi through which individual power is developed and applied to the economic problems of life.

If you organize your own faculties after the pattern laid down in this Ladder, by properly developing the qualities represented by the sixteen rungs, you will find your power enormously increased. You will find yourself in possession of power that you did not know you possessed, and through the intelligent direction of this power you can attain practically any position in life to which you aspire.

The sixteen rungs of this ladder represent the choicest and the most illustrative experience of my twenty-two years of business life:

Rung No. 1: A Definite Aim in Life

Rung No. 2: Self-Confidence

Rung No. 3: Initiative

Rung No. 4: Imagination

Rung No. 5: Action

Rung No. 6: Enthusiasm

Rung No. 7: Self-Control

Rung No. 8: The Habit of Performing More Work and Better Work Than You Are Paid to Perform

Rung No. 9: An Attractive Personality

Rung No. 10: Accurate Thought

Rung No. 11: Concentration

Rung No. 12: Persistence

Rung No. 13: Failures

Rung No. 14: Tolerance and Sympathy

Rung No. 15: Work

Rung No. 16: The Golden Rule

I will take you behind the curtains of my own private life so that you may learn these great lessons, as portrayed in the outline of the Ladder, with the hope that the road you will have to travel to reach your objective may be somewhat shortened, and the obstacles that surely await you somewhat minimized.

Success ought not to be a mere matter of chance, as is true in the majority of instances, because the roadway over which success is reached is now well known, and every inch of it has been carefully and accurately charted. The Magic Ladder to Success will carry you wherever you wish to go if you will master it and organize your faculties according to its plan—a statement I make after having not only organized my own faculties and directed them to a given end successfully, but after having helped others to do the same in many thousands of cases.

This Magic Ladder to Success represents twenty-two years of actual experience and observation, at least twelve of which have been directed to the intense analysis and study of character and human conduct.

During the past twelve years I have analyzed more than 12,000 men and women. These analyses developed some startling facts, one of which was that 95 percent of the adult population belongs to the class that might properly be called unorganized (both as to individual faculties and as to group or collective effort), or followers, and the other five percent might be called leaders. Another startling fact discovered from organizing and classifying the tendencies and habits of human beings, as shown by these analyses, was that the main reason why the overwhelmingly large percentage of people belonged in the class of followers was lack of a definite purpose in life and a definite plan for carrying out that purpose.

With the foregoing analysis of the Magic Ladder to Success, you have already seen that the ladder deals entirely with the subject of acquiring human power through organization, coordination, and classification of the human faculties. Bear in mind that this Ladder is not intended as a panacea for all the evils that beset the pathway of the human race, neither is it intended as a "new" formula for success. Its purpose is to help you organize what you already have and direct your efforts in the future more powerfully and more accurately than you have done in the past. Its purpose, stated in another way, is to help you educate yourself. By the word educate I mean to develop, organize, and intelligently direct the natural faculties present in what is called the mind.

Power comes through real education! No person is educated who has not learned to organize, classify, and intelligently direct the faculties of the mind to a definite end. No person is educated who has not learned to separate facts from mere information, weaving the facts into an organized plan of action, with a definite objective in view.

Mere schooling is no evidence of education. College degrees are no evidence that those holding them are persons of education. The word educate comes, if I recall correctly, from the Latin word *educo*, meaning to develop from within, to educe, to draw out, to expand through use. It does not mean to cram the brain with knowledge, as most dictionaries tell us it does.

I dwell at length on the words *educate* and *organize*, because these two words are the very foundation, the very warp and woof of the Magic Ladder to Success.

Education is something you must acquire. No one can give it to you; you must get it for yourself. You have to work to get it and you have to work to keep it. Education comes not from knowing but from doing. Every library is full of facts, but the books themselves have no power. They are not educated because they cannot put into action the facts that have been classified and filed away in their pages. So it is with the human automaton that merely gathers knowledge and makes no organized use of it.

There is considerable energy in a ton of coal, but the coal must first be dug out of the ground and put into action, through the aid of combustion, before that energy can be utilized. What is merely latent in the human brain represents no more energy or power than does the coal under the ground, until it is organized and put into action to some definite end.

The reason that people can acquire an education through the cooperation of schools and teachers more readily than they can acquire it without these is the fact that schools help to organize knowledge. If I seem to lay undue stress upon this question of organization, let me remind you that the lack of this very ability to organize, classify, and intelligently direct the faculties of the mind constitutes the rocks and reefs on which a large majority of the "failures" flounder and go down to ruin.

If, through repetition and by approaching this question from various angles, as I have intended to do, I can drive home the importance of properly organizing your faculties and directing them to a definite end, I will have done for you all that any school on earth aims to do for its students.

With the foregoing as a prelude, we are now ready to take up the first rung of the Magic Ladder to Success.

Rung No. 1:
A Definite Aim In Life

No one would think of gathering together a quantity of sand, lumber, brick, and building materials with the object of building a house without first creating a definite plan for that house, yet my experience in analyzing over 12,000 people proved conclusively that 95 percent of the people have no such plan for building a career, which is a thousand times more important than the building of a house.

Do not overlook the significance of the word *definite*, because it is the most important word in the phrase "a definite aim in life." Without this word, the sentence represents what we all have, which is nothing more than a vague aim to succeed. How, when, or where, we know not, or at least those of us who belong to the 95 percent class do not. We resemble a ship without a rudder, floundering on the ocean, running around in circles and using up energy that never carries us to shore because we do not aim toward one definite goal and carry on until we reach it.

You are beginning now to acquire human power through the organization, classification, and intelligent direction of knowledge, but your first step must be the choice of a definite aim or else you might as well have no power, since you will not be able to guide it to a worthwhile objective. It is necessary, not only to have a definite aim in life, but you must also have a definite plan for attaining that aim. Therefore, place on paper a written statement of your definite aim and also a written statement, in as much detail as possible, of your plan for attaining that aim.

There is a psychological reason for insisting that you reduce your definite aim and your plan for attaining it to writing, a reason you will thoroughly understand after you have mastered the subject of auto-suggestion.

Bear in mind that both your definite aim and your plan for attaining it may be modified from time to time. As a matter of fact, you will be an unusual person if you have the vision and the imagination to see a definite aim now that will be large enough in its scope to satisfy your ambition a little later on. The important thing for you to do now is to learn the significance of working always with a definite aim in view, and always with a definite plan. This principle is one that you must make a part of the process of organizing your faculties, and you must apply it in everything you do, thus forming the habit of systematic, organized effort.

One year from the time that you write out your first statement of your definite aim in life, you will be surprised, more than likely, at the small scope it covered, for you will then have developed greater vision and greater self-confidence. You will be able to accomplish more because of your belief that you can do so and because of your courage in setting a bigger task for yourself, as indicated by your definite aim.

This process of education—of *educing*, expanding from within, and drawing out your mind— will enable you to think in bigger terms without becoming frightened. It will enable you to look upon your definite aim in life with eyes of analysis and synthesis, and to see it not only in its entirety but in its component parts, all of which will seem small and insignificant to you. Engineers move mountains from one spot to another with no difficulty whatsoever, not by trying to move the whole mountain with one shovelful, but by one shovelful at a time and according to a definite plan.

The time and the necessary money required to build the Panama Canal were correctly estimated years ahead, in fact before a single shovelful of dirt had been removed, because the engineers who built it had learned how to work by definite plans.

The Canal was a success!

It was a success because the people who planned and built it followed the principle that I have laid down, for your guidance, as the first rung in this ladder. Therefore you can readily see that there is nothing new about this principle. It needs no experiment to prove its accuracy because the successful people of the past have already proved this.

Make up your mind now what you wish to do in life, then formulate your plans and commence doing it. If you have trouble deciding what your lifework ought to be, you can secure the services of able coaches and guides who can assist you in selecting a lifework that will be in harmony with your natural inclinations, your temperament, physical strength, training, and native ability.

This brings us to the second rung in the Ladder.

Rung No. 2: Self-Confidence

It would hardly be worthwhile to create a definite aim in life or a plan for attaining it unless one possessed the self-confidence with which to put the plan into action and achieve the aim. Nearly everyone has a certain amount of what is ordinarily considered self-confidence, but only a relatively small number possess the particular kind of self-confidence that we name as the second rung in the Magic Ladder to Success.

Self-confidence is a state of mind that anyone can develop in a short period of time. Twenty-odd years ago I was engaged as a laborer in the coalmines. I was without a definite aim and lacked the self-confidence necessary to create such an aim. Something happened one night that marked the most important turning point in my life. I was sitting before an open fire, discussing with a companion the problem of unrest and antagonism between employer and employee. I said something that impressed this man and he did something that gave me my first lesson in self-confidence building. He then reached over, took me by the shoulder, looked me squarely in the eye, and said, "Why, you are a bright boy, and if you will get out and go to school, you will make your mark in the world!"

It was not what he said as much as it was the manner in which he said it—the sparkle in his eye, the firmness with which he gripped my shoulder as he spoke—that impressed me. It was the first time in my life that anyone had told me I was "bright," or that I might make my "mark" in the world. It gave me my first ray of hope, my first fleeting glimpse of self-confidence.

The seed of self-confidence was sown in my mind on that occasion and it has been growing all these years. The first thing this planting in my mind of the seed of self-confidence did was to cause me to break away from the mines and enter more remunerative work. It caused me to become thirsty for knowledge, so much so that I am becoming a more efficient student every year that I live, until today I can gather, classify, and organize facts in less than one-tenth the time I required only a few years ago.

Rung No. 3: Initiative

Initiative is that very rare quality that impels a person to do what ought to be done without being told to do it. All great leaders must possess initiative. A person without initiative could never become a great general, either in warfare or in business and industry, because generalship, to be successful, must be based on intense action.

Golden opportunities are lurking at every corner, waiting for the person with initiative to come along and discover them. When people perform only the tasks allotted to them and then stop, they attract no particular attention. But when they take the initiative, go ahead and look for other tasks to be performed after their regular duties have been taken care of, they attract the favorable attention of their superiors who willingly allot to them greater responsibilities, with pay accordingly.

Before anyone can rise very high in any field of endeavor, he or she must become a person of vision who can think in big terms, who can create definite plans and then carry these plans into action, all of which makes it imperative that the quality of initiative be developed.

You might have noticed already that one of the significant features concerning this Magic Ladder is the extent to which its rungs blend and harmonize with one another, to the end that the whole Ladder constitutes a powerful organization of usable material. Notice how the third and fourth rungs complement each other, for instance, and notice also the power that comes out of a proper blending of these two rungs in the practical affairs of life.

Rung No. 4: Imagination

Imagination is the workshop of the human mind in which old ideas are built into new combinations and new plans. When Thomas Edison invented the incandescent light, he merely brought together, in his imagination first and then in his laboratory, two well-known principles and hooked them up, so to speak, in a new way. He knew, as almost every amateur electrician knows, that friction in an electric line would cause heat; that the line could be heated, at the point of friction, to a white glow and thereby produce light. But the trouble was that the wire would burn in two.

Finally, after searching all over the world for a special fiber or filament that could be heated to a white glow without its burning in two, Edison thought of the old charcoal principle, wherein a pile of wood is placed on the ground, set on fire, and then covered over with dirt and the air cut off. The wood smolders along, but it cannot burn up entirely because most of the oxygen has been cut off, and there can be, therefore, not enough combustion. The moment Edison thought of this charcoal principle, he went into his laboratory, placed the filament inside of a globe, cut off the air, and lo and behold he produced the long sought incandescent light.

When Christopher Columbus turned his eyes westward in search of a "new world," he made the most profitable use of initiative and imagination ever recorded in all history. Out of his blending of these two qualities was born America.

When Gutenberg turned his attention to the invention of the modern printing press, he also made profitable use of initiative and imagination, because he gave wings to thought and brought the whole world closer.

When the Wright brothers turned their attention to the airplane, they used initiative and imagination, which, within the span of a few years, mastered the air and shortened the distance between two given points by an enormous proportion.

All of the great inventions owe their existence to the blending of these two forces—initiative and imagination. The limits to which a person of ordinary ability can attain, through the use of initiative and imagination, no person can define. Lack of these two qualities is the main reason why 95 percent of the adult people of the world have no definite aim in life, which, in turn, is also the reason why this same 95 percent constitute the followers in life.

Leaders are always men and women of initiative and imagination.

Rung No. 5:
Action

The world pays for only one thing and that is for service rendered, or in other words, action. Stored-away knowledge is worthless. It benefits no one until it has been expressed in terms of action. No one pays for goods on the shelves; they must be hauled down and ushered into service before the world pays for them.

You might be a graduate of one of the best colleges or universities—in fact, you might have all the facts in all of the encyclopedias in the world stored away in your head—but unless you organize this knowledge and express it in action, it would be worth nothing to you or to the world.

A few years ago I went out into the Chicago public parks and interviewed seven of the homeless—those fellows who lie around, asleep, with newspapers over their faces while work is plentiful and wages high. I wanted to catch a glimpse of their particular "alibi." I knew they had what they believed to be a "reason" for being without work.

With some small change and a pocket full of cigars, I got pretty close to these fellows, and what do you suppose they told me, every single one of them?

Each of them said substantially this: "I am here because the world would not give me a chance!"

Think of it—"because the world would not give me a chance!"

Did the world ever give any person a chance, other than what one went out and created by the use of their imagination, self-confidence, initiative, and those other qualities mentioned in this Ladder? We need not argue the point that if there is no action, all the education in the world, all the knowledge that ever came from the best colleges and universities on earth, and all the good intentions plus all of the other qualities mentioned in this magic ladder, will not be of any value whatsoever.

A person without this great quality of action resembles a great locomotive that stands on the side track or in the roundhouse with coal in the bunker, water in the tank, fire in the firebox, steam in the dome, but no engineer to open the throttle. This great piece of locomotive power is as useless as a sand dune until someone opens the throttle and puts the thing into action.

Within that head of yours is a great machine, one that rivals all the locomotives and manmade machines ever built, but it is as useless as the locomotive that stands on the side of the track without the engineer, until you put it into action. How many millions of people are there in this world who have all the essentials for great success, who have everything necessary with which to render the world a great service, except one quality—action!

With but little use of your imagination you can see how closely related action is to all of the other qualities covered by the first four rungs in the ladder. You can see how the lack of action would nullify all of the other qualities. When a person goes into action, those negative qualities of procrastination, fear, worry, and doubt are strictly on the defensive, and nearly everyone knows that a better fight can be fought on the offensive than can be fought on the defensive.

Action is one of the chief qualities that all leaders must possess and, incidentally, it is the chief quality that distinguishes the leader from those who follow. This is worth thinking about; it may help some of us advance from the rank and file of the followers into the select, limited class who are leaders.

Rung No. 6: Enthusiasm

The next rung in the Ladder is very appropriately called enthusiasm, because enthusiasm usually arouses one to action and therefore should be closely associated with it. If we were considering the steps of this Ladder in the order of their importance, probably enthusiasm would precede action because there is not apt to be very much action in a person unless there is enthusiasm.

Enthusiasm usually develops automatically, when people find the work for which they are best fitted; the work they like best. It is not likely that you will be able to maintain very much enthusiasm over work you dislike, therefore it behooves you to search diligently until you find the work into which you can throw your whole heart and soul—the work in which you can earnestly and persistently "lose" yourself.

Rung No. 7: Self-Control

For eighteen long, perilous years, an archenemy stood between me and the attainment of my definite aim.

That enemy was lack of self-control.

I was always looking for controversy and argument. Usually I found it. Most of my time was spent in showing someone that he or she was wrong, when I should have been devoting this valuable time to showing myself that I was wrong. Finding fault with people is undoubtedly the most unprofitable business one ever engages in. It makes enemies and demoralizes the spirit of friendship. In no way does it reform or help another person.

Lack of self-control leads to fault-finding.

No one ever became a great leader of others until first learning to lead himself or herself through self-control. Self-mastery is the first stepping stone to real achievement. When people lose their tempers, something takes place in their brains that ought to be understood more generally. Angry people do not really "lose" their tempers, they merely inflame it and cause it to draw to the brain those chemicals which, when combined through anger, form a deadly poison.

An angry person will throw off enough poison, with every exhalation of breath, to kill a guinea pig!

There are only three ways of getting rid of the poison manufactured by the brain in anger. One is through the pores of the skin; one is through the lungs, the poison being carried away on the breath in the form of gases; and the other is through the liver, which separates the waste matter from the blood.

When these three roadways become overworked, the surplus poison being manufactured by an angry person is distributed through the system and poisons it, just as if any other deadly and poisonous drug were injected into the blood with the use of a hypodermic syringe. Anger, hatred, cynicism, pessimism, and other negative states of mind tend to poison the system and should be avoided. They are all a part of that deadly negative called lack of self-control.

Rung No. 8:
The Habit of Performing More Work and Better Work Than You Are Paid to Perform

I do not believe it possible for anyone to rise above mediocrity without developing this habit of performing more service and better service than is actually paid for in dollars and cents. The person who makes it a habit to do this is usually regarded as a leader, and without exception, as far as we know, all such people have risen to the top in their profession or business, regardless of other handicaps that may have stood in the way.

A person who renders this sort of service is sure to attract the attention of people who will start a lively competition for his or her services. No one ever heard of competition over the services of the person who performs as little work as possible, and who performs that work in a careless manner in an unwilling spirit.

All of the ability on earth, all of the knowledge recorded in all of the books down the ages, all the schooling on earth, will not create a profitable market for the services of a man or woman who renders as little service as possible and makes the quality as poor as will pass.

On the other hand, the spirit of willingly performing more work and better work than one is paid to perform is sure to bring its just reward. It will offset many other negative qualities and the lack of many other desirable qualities.

Rung No. 9:
An Attractive Personality

You can readily see that even though you possess all of the qualities thus far outlined, you would nevertheless be very apt to fail in your lifework if you did not also attract people to you through a pleasing personality.

Personality cannot be defined in one word, because it is the sum total of those qualities that distinguish one person from every other person on earth. The clothes you wear form a part of your personality—a very important part at that. Your facial expression, as shown by the lines on your face or the lack of these, forms a part of your personality. The words you speak form a very important part of your personality, and mark you instantly, once you have spoken, as a person of refinement or the opposite. Your voice also constitutes an important part of your personality, a part which, to be pleasing, must be cultivated, trained, and developed so it is harmonious, rich, and expressed with rhythm. The manner in which you shake hands forms an important part of your personality; therefore, make your handshake firm and vibrant. If you merely permit the other person to shake your limp, cold, lifeless hand, you are displaying what constitutes a negative personality.

An attractive personality may be described as one that draws people to you and causes them to find companionship and harmony in your company, while an unattractive personality is one that causes people to want to get as far away from you as possible.

You undoubtedly can analyze yourself and determine whether or not people are attracted to you, and if they are not, you surely can find the reason why. Also, it may be of interest to you to know that the class of people you attract to yourself clearly indicates your own character and personality, because you will attract only those who are in harmony with you and whose characters and nature correspond to that of your own.

An attractive personality usually may be found in the person who speaks gently and kindly, selecting words that do not offend; who selects clothing of appropriate style, and colors that harmonize. The person who is unselfish and willing to serve others; who is a friend of all humanity, regardless of politics, religion, creed, or economic viewpoints; who refrains from speaking unkindly of others, either with or without cause. The person who manages to converse without being drawn into an argument or trying to draw others into argument on such debatable subjects as religion and politics; who sees the good there is in people and overlooks the bad; who seeks neither to reform nor reprimand others; who smiles frequently and deeply. The person who loves little children, flowers, birds, the growing grass, the trees, and the running brooks; who sympathizes with all who are in trouble; who forgives acts of unkindness; who willingly grants to others the rights to do as they please as long as no one else's rights are interfered with. The person who earnestly strives to be constructive in every thought and act; who encourages others and spurs them on to greater undertakings in some useful work for the good of humanity, by interesting them in themselves and inspiring them with self-confidence; who is a patient and interested listener and makes a habit of giving the other person a part of the conversation without breaking in and doing all the talking.

An attractive personality, like all of the other qualities mentioned in this Ladder, is easily developed through the application of applied psychology.

Rung No. 10: Accurate Thought

After you have learned how to think correctly, you will easily and automatically practice the habit of examining everything that tries to make its way to your mind, to see whether it is mere "information" or facts. You will learn how to keep away from your mind all those sense impressions that arise, not from facts but from prejudices and from hatred, anger, bias, and other false sources.

You will learn how to separate facts into two groups, namely the relevant and irrelevant, or the important and unimportant. You will learn how to take the "important" facts and organize them, working them into a perfect judgment or plan of action.

You will learn how to analyze what you read or see through various media outlets, making the necessary deductions, reasoning from the known facts to the unknown, and arriving at a well-balanced judgment that is not colored by prejudice or built out of mere "information" that you did not carefully examine.

You will also learn, when you understand how to think correctly, how to put what others say through the same process, because this will lead you nearer to the truth. You will learn not to take anything for a fact unless it squares up with your own intelligence, and unless it meets the various tests to which a sound thinker always subjects everything that tries to make its way to his or her mind.

You will learn, also, not to be influenced by what one person says about another, until you have weighed the statement, examined it, and determined, according to the known principles of correct thinking, whether the statement is false or true.

If scientific thinking will do all of this for you, it is a desirable quality, is it not?

It will do all of this—and much more—when you understand the comparatively simple principles through which correct thought is produced.

Rung No. 11: Concentration

Concentration, in the sense that we have made it one of the rungs of this Ladder, has reference to the practice of inducing your mind to picture all of the details outlined in your chief aim or in any undertaking, whether connected with or leading to your chief aim or not, until that picture has been clearly outlined and practical ways and means of transforming it into reality have been created.

Concentration is the process of causing your imagination to search every crevice and corner of your subconscious mind, wherein is stored away a perfect picture of every sense impression that ever reached your mind through your five senses, and finding all that can be used in connection with the object of the concentration.

Concentration is also the process of bringing together, as electric batteries are connected by wires, the combined strength of all the qualities outlined in this Ladder for the purpose of achieving a given end or attaining a given object— the object of the concentration.

It is the process of focusing the powers of thought upon a given subject until the mind has analyzed that subject and separated it into its component parts, then reassembled it again into a definite plan.

It is the process of studying effects by their causes and, conversely, causes by their effects.

Rung No. 12: Persistence

Persistence and concentration are so closely related that it is hard to say where is the line that separates them.

Persistence is synonymous with will power or determination. It is the quality that causes you to keep the powers of your mind focused upon a given objective, through the principle of concentration, until that objective has been reached.

Persistence is the quality that causes you to arise, when once you have been knocked down by temporary failure, and to continue your pursuit of a given desire or object. It is the quality that gives you courage and faith to keep on trying in the face of any and all obstacles that may confront you.

It is the quality that causes the bulldog to find the death grip on his opponent's throat and then lie down and hold on in spite of all efforts to shake him off.

However, you are not aiming to develop persistence for the purpose of using it as a bulldog does. You are developing it for the purpose of carrying you over those necessary rocks and reefs that nearly every person must master in reaching any worthwhile place in the world. You are developing persistence to guide you, unwavering, in a given direction only after you are satisfied that you are going in the right direction. Indiscriminate use of persistence, however, might only get you in trouble.

Rung No. 13: Failures

This brings us to the "lucky" thirteenth rung of the Ladder—failures!

Do not stumble on this rung. It is the most interesting rung of all because it deals with facts that you must face in life, whether you wish to do so or not. It shows you, as clearly as you might see the sun on a clear day, how you can turn every failure into an asset; how you can carve every failure into a foundation stone upon which your house of success will stand forever.

Failure is the only subject in the whole Ladder that might be called "negative," and I shall show you how and why it is one of the most important of life's experiences.

Failure is nature's plan of hurdle-jumping and training people for a worthwhile work in life. It is nature's great crucible and tempering process that burns the dross from all the other human qualities and purifies the metal so it will withstand all hard usage throughout life. Failure is the great law of resistance that makes people stronger in proportion to the extent that they overcome this resistance.

In every failure there is a great and lasting lesson, if one will only analyze, think, and profit by it. Failure develops tolerance, sympathy, and kindness in the human heart.

You will not travel very far down life's pathway before you discover that every adversity and every failure is a blessing in disguise, a blessing because it has put your mind and your body into action and thereby caused both to grow through the law of use.

Look back down the ages and you will find history full of incidents that show clearly the cleansing, purifying, strengthening value of failure.

When you begin to realize that failure is a necessary part of one's education, you will no longer look upon it with fear, and the first thing you know, there will be no more failures! No person ever arose from the knockout blow of defeat without being a stronger and wiser human being in one respect or another.

If you will look back over your own failures, if you are fortunate enough to be able to point to any of very great consequence, you will no doubt see that those failures marked certain turning points in your life and in your plans that were of benefit to you.

Rung No. 14: Tolerance and Sympathy

One of the curses of this world today is intolerance and a lack of sympathy.

Had the world been tolerant, wars would never have swept the face of the civilized globe as they have. Here in America, it is of particular importance that we learn the lesson of tolerance and sympathy, for the reason that this is a great melting pot in which we are living side by side with every race and with the followers of every creed and religion on earth.

Unless we display tolerance and sympathy, we are not living up to the standard that first distinguished this from the tyrant's world across the Atlantic. Many great lessons can be learned from wars, but none more importance than this: that the followers of all religions and all nationalities and races have fought for a common cause.

If we could fight for a common cause during a war, without displaying intolerance for one another on account of religion, race, and creed, and if we found it necessary and profitable to do so, why not continue to do the same in peace?

Power comes out of cooperation!

All through the ages, struggling people have suffered more from their own gross indifference and violent intolerance with one another than they have from oppression by the ruling classes. As a matter of fact, if the common people could lay aside intolerance and work for a common cause, behind a solid front, no power on earth could defeat them.

In warfare, defeat usually comes from lack of organization. The same is true in life. Intolerance and lack of harmonious effort toward a common end has always left the door open, so that a few who understood the power that comes from organized effort might step right in and ride the backs of the disorganized and the intolerant.

Just now, intolerance is working havoc with the world, because of terrorism and religion. These disagreements are nothing but intolerance and greed, and it is as much in evidence on one side as it is on the other. If both sides would see that one is the arm while the other is the lifeblood keeping that arm alive, each would see that intolerance that affects one adversely also affects the other in the same way.

Let us be done with intolerance by placing principle above religion, humanity and the selfish individual. Let us exercise at least as much real intelligence as does the little honeybee that works for the good of the hive, that the hive may not perish.

Rung No. 15: Work

This is the shortest word of all those that constitute the rungs of this Ladder, yet it is one of the most important of qualities.

All of nature's laws have decreed that nothing may live that is not used. The arm that is tied to one's side and removed from active use will wither up and perish away. So it is with any other part of the physical body. Disuse brings decay and death. Likewise the human mind, with all of its qualities, will not wither up and decay unless it is used, but the brain, the physical agent through which the mind functions, will decay.

Every picture that reaches the human brain through the five senses embeds itself upon one of the tiny brain cells, there to wither up and die through disuse or to become vivid and healthy through constant use. Educators now concede that it is not the actual knowledge children gather from schoolbooks that constitutes their "education." It is the brain development that takes place in the process of transferring that knowledge from the books to the brain, bringing a corresponding amount of use of the brain itself, which constitutes the real value of schooling.

The qualities outlined in this Ladder are yours in return for just one price, and that price is work—persistent, never-ceasing work. As long as you exercise these qualities and keep them at work, they will be strong and healthy. But if you permit them to lie dormant, unused, they will wither into decay and finally into death.

Rung No. 16:
The Golden Rule

This is the last rung of the Ladder. Perhaps it should have been the first rung, because its use or disuse will determine whether one ultimately fails or succeeds in the application of all the other qualities mentioned in the ladder. This Golden Rule philosophy is the shining sun that should form the background of all the other qualities outlined in the Ladder. Unless the Golden Rule lights the pathway over which you travel, you are apt to plunge headlong into pitfalls from which you can never escape.

The Golden Rule offers the only sure roadway to happiness, because it leads straight through the field of useful service in the interest of humanity. It is the thing that develops the "hive" spirit in people and causes them to submerge their selfish personal interests for the good of the race.

The Golden Rule acts as a barrier to all of our tendencies toward wielding the destructive use of power that results from developing the other qualities outlined in this Ladder. It is the antidote against the harm people can do without knowledge and power, the thing that guides people to the intelligent, constructive use of those qualities we develop from the use of the rungs of this Ladder.

The Golden Rule is the torchlight by which we are guided toward those objectives in life that leave something of value to posterity, that lightens the burdens of our fellow sojourners on earth and helps them find the way to useful, constructive effort.

The Golden Rule simply means that we must act toward others as we wish others to act toward us; that we must do unto them as we wish to be done unto us; that we must give in thoughts, actions, and deeds that which we are willing to receive from others.

You have before you, in this Ladder, a perfect blueprint or plan by which you can reach any legitimate undertaking in life that is within possible reach of a person of your age, natural tendency, schooling, and environment. This is a Magic Ladder to guide you to look for the end of the rainbow of success—which nearly all of us expect to find at some point in life.

Your rainbow's end is in sight, and the moment you master the qualities in this Ladder, you can pick up the bag of gold that is waiting there for the rightful owner to come along and claim it.

FOUR

Why Some People Succeed: One Secret

I have made an important discovery—a discovery that may help you, whoever you are, whatever may be your aim in life, to achieve success.

It is not the touch of genius that some people are supposed to be gifted with, that brings success. It is not good luck, influence, or wealth.

The real thing upon which most great fortunes were built—the thing that helps men and women rise to fame and high position in the world—is easily described:

It is simply the habit of completing everything one begins, first having learned what to begin and what not to begin.

Take inventory of yourself over the past two years, let us say, and what do you discover? The chances are about fifty to one that you will discover you have had many ideas, started many plans, but completed few or none of them.

In the series of lessons on applied psychology you will find one explaining the importance of concentration, followed by simple, explicit information on exactly how to learn to concentrate.

You will do well to look that particular lesson up and study it over again. Study it with a new idea in mind—that of learning how to complete all that you undertake.

You have heard it stated, ever since you were old enough to remember, that "procrastination is the thief of time." But because it seemed like preaching, you paid no attention to it.

That axiom is literally true!

THE POWER OF SIMPLY STICKING TO IT

You cannot possibly succeed in any undertaking, whether it is large or small, important or otherwise, if you merely think of what you would like to accomplish and then sit down and wait for the thing to materialize without patient, painstaking effort.

Nearly every business that stands out above the common run of similar businesses represents concentration on a definite plan or idea from which there has been but little, if any, variance.

Fast food chains, for instance, are built upon a definite plan through the principle of concentration—the plan itself being simple and easily applied to other lines of business.

The automobile business is nothing more than concentration upon a simple plan, that is to give the public a serviceable car with good mileage for as little money as possible, giving the buyer the advantage of quantity production.

The great mail-order houses represent sine of the largest merchandising enterprises in the world—having been built upon the simple plan of giving the buyer the advantage of quantity buying and selling, and the policy of either satisfying the customers or giving their money back

There are other examples of great merchandising success that were built upon the same principle—adopting a definite plan and then sticking to it to the end.

However, for every great success to which we can point as a result of this principle, we can find a thousand failures or near failures where no such plan has been adopted.

HALF-BAKED IDEAS DON'T RISE

I was recently talking with a man—a man who is bright and, in many ways, a capable businessman, but he is not succeeding for the simple reason that he has too many half-baked ideas and follows the practice of discarding all of them before they have been fairly tested.

I offered him a suggestion that might have been valuable to him, but he replied immediately, "Oh, I've thought of that several times, and I started to try it out once, but it didn't work."

Note the words well: "I started to try it out once, but it didn't work." Ah, there was where the weakness might have been discovered. He "started" to try it out.

Readers of the Golden Rule, mark these words: It is not the person who merely "starts" a thing who succeeds. It is the person who starts and who finishes in spite of hell!

Anybody can start a task. It takes the so-called genius to muster up enough courage, self-confidence, and painstaking patience to finish.

But this is not "genius;" it is nothing but persistence and good common sense. The person who is accredited with being a genius usually is, as Edison so often told us, nothing of the kind—that person is merely a hard worker who finds a sound plan and then sticks to it.

Success rarely—if ever—comes all in a bunch, or in a hurry. Worthwhile achievement usually represents long and patient service.

Remember the sturdy oak tree. It does not grow in a year, or in two or even three years. It requires a score of years or more to produce a fair-sized oak tree. There are trees that will grow very large in a few years, but their wood is soft and porous and they are short-lived trees.

The person who decides to be a chef this year, then changes his or her mind and tries the financial business the next year, and then switches again to life insurance the third year, is more apt to be a failure at all three, whereas sticking to one of these for three years might have built a very fair success.

WHY I KNOW THIS MISTAKE SO WELL

You see, I know a great deal about what I am writing because I made this very same mistake for almost fifteen years. I feel that I have a perfectly good right to warn you of an obstacle that may beset your pathway because I have suffered many defeats on account of that hurdle and consequently have learned how to recognize it in you.

The first of January—the day for good resolutions—is nearing. Set aside that day for two purposes, and you will be quite likely to profit by having read this article.

First: Adopt a chief aim for yourself for the next year at least and preferably for the next five years, and write out that aim word by word.

Second: Determine to make the first plank in that chief aim platform read something like this: "During the ensuing year I will determine, as nearly as possible, those tasks I shall have to perform from start to finish in order to be successful, and nothing under the sun shall divert my efforts from finishing every task I begin."

Nearly every person has intelligence enough to create ideas, but the trouble with most is that those ideas never find expression in action. The finest locomotive on earth is not worth a shilling, nor will it pull a single pound of weight, until the stored-up energy in the steam dome is released at the throttle.

You have energy in that head of yours—every normal human being has—but you are not releasing it at the throttle of action! You are not applying it through the principle of concentration to the tasks, which, if completed, would place you on the list of those who are regarded as successes.

As far as I can determine, the chief objection to alcohol is the indisputable fact that it has a very decided tendency to render the human mind "dopey" and inactive. This is enough to condemn it, because anything that retards a person's action, or the releasing of ability through the habit of concentrating the mind on a task until it is finished, is detrimental to his or her welfare.

Usually people will release the flow of action that has stored up in their heads in connection with a task they delight in performing. This is the reason why people ought to engage in the work they like best.

There is a way of coaxing that wonderful mind of yours to give up its energy and pour it out into action through concentration upon some useful work. Keep on searching until you find the best possible way of releasing this energy. Find the work through which you can release this energy most readily and most willingly, and you will be getting mighty near to the work in which you ought to find success.

GENIUS ISN'T WHAT WE THINK

It has been my privilege to interview many so-called great people—people who have been regarded as "geniuses"—and, as encouragement to you, I want to tell you frankly that I found nothing in them that you and I and all of the other "ordinary" people do not possess. They are exactly like us, with no more brains—sometimes with less—but what they had that you and I also have, but do not always use, was the ability to release the action that was stored up in their heads and keep it concentrated on a task, great or small, until completed.

Do not expect to become an adept at concentration the first time you try. Learn first to concentrate upon the little things you do—the sharpening of a pencil, the wrapping of a package, the typing of a message, and so forth.

The way to attain perfection in this wonderful art of finishing all that you start is to form the habit of doing this in connection with every task you perform, no matter how small.

The first thing you know, this becomes a regular habit and you do it automatically, without effort.

Of what importance will this be to you?

What a useless, silly question—but listen and I shall answer: It will mean the difference between failure and success!

FIVE

My Life's
Seven Turning Points

This is a narrative of my experience, covering a period of more than twenty years. It shows how necessary it is to take the long view in order to arrive at the vital truths of life and interpret the silent workings of the unseen hand that guides our destinies. The significance of this recounting lies not in any single event, but in the interpretation of all the events and their relationship with one another.

PRELUDE

There is a legend, as old as the human race, which tells us that a pot of gold may be found at the end of a rainbow.

This fairy tale, which grips the imagination, may have something to do with the present tendency of the race to worship at the shrine of Mammon.

For nearly fifteen years I sought the end of my rainbow, that I might claim the pot of gold. My struggle in search of the evasive rainbow's end was ceaseless. It carried me up the mountainsides of failure and down the hillsides of despair, luring me on and on in search of the phantom pot of gold.

Lay aside your cares and come with me while I paint a word picture of the winding pathway I took. I shall show you the seven important turning points of my life. Perhaps I can help you shorten the distance to your rainbow's end. For the present, I will confine my narrative to the simple details of what I experienced in my search, as it carried me, time and time again, almost within reach of the coveted goal, and then snatched it away from me.

As you retrace my footsteps with me, you will see furrows of experience that have been plowed with thorns and watered with tears; you will walk with me down through the "Valley of the Shadow;" you will scale the mountaintops of expectation and find yourself suddenly crashing to the bottomless pits of despondency and failure; you will walk through green fields and crawl over sandy deserts.

Finally, we will arrive at the rainbow's end!

Be prepared for a shock, because you will see not only the pot of gold that legends of the past have foretold, but you will find something else that is more to be coveted than all the gold on earth. Finding out what this "something" is shall be your reward for following me in this word picture.

One morning I was awakened abruptly, as if someone had shaken me. I looked around and found no one in the room. It was 3 am. In the fractional part of a minute, I saw a clear, concise picture that epitomized the seven turning points of my life, just as they are here described. I felt an impelling desire—it was much more than a desire; it was a command—to reduce the picture to words and use it as a public lecture.

Until this moment I had failed, utterly, to correctly interpret many of my life's experiences, some of which had left scars of disappointment on my heart and a touch of bitterness that somewhat colored and modified my efforts to be a constructive servant of the people.

You will pardon me if I refrain from expressing the real feelings I had during the moment when the last lingering touch of intolerance was wiped out of my heart, and I saw, for the first time in my life, the real significance of those trying experiences, those heartaches, those disappointments, and those hardships that overtake all of us at one time or another. I ask that you pardon me for omitting the description of my *real* feelings on this occasion, not only because of the sacredness of the experience, but because of lack of words with which to correctly interpret those feelings.

With this foundation, you may come with me to the beginning of the first important turning point in my life, which happened more than twenty years ago while I was a homeless lad without education and without an aim in life. I was floating helplessly on the sea of life, as a dry leaf would float on the bosom of the winds. As well as I can remember, no ambition higher than that of being a laborer in the coal mines had ever reached my mind. The hand of fate seemed to be against me. I believed in no one except God and myself, and sometimes I wondered if God were not double-crossing me!

I was cynical and filled with skepticism and doubt. I believed in nothing that I couldn't understand. Two and two meant four to me only when I put down the figures and had done the adding myself.

All of which, I freely admit, is a prosaic, uneventful beginning for this narrative, a fact for which I am in no way responsible, since I am here setting down only what happened. And may it not be well if I here digress just a moment while I remind you that most early-life experiences are uneventful, dry, and prosaic. This point seems so vital that I feel impelled to turn the spotlight on it before I proceed with my narrative, that it may become an illuminating factor in helping you to interpret the experiences of your own life in the light of the real significance of every event, no matter how insignificant it may have seemed at the time.

I am convinced that too often we look for the important events in life to come in a dramatic, impressive, and staged manner, whereas in reality they come and go unnoticed except for the joy and grief that they bring, and we lose sight of the real lessons they teach while we fix our attention upon this joy or grief.

The event of which I now write happened just twenty years ago.

MY LIFE'S FIRST TURNING POINT

The first turning point was one I discuss elsewhere, having to do with a spontaneous remark addressed to me by an older worker, pointing out that I was a bright boy and should I stay in school, I would be successful.

The first concrete result of that remark caused me to enroll for a course in a business college, a step that I am duty-bound to admit proved to be one of the most helpful I ever took, because I got my first fleeting glimpse, in my business college training, of what one might call a fair sense of proportions. Here I learned the spirit of simple democracy and, most important of all, I got hold of the idea that it would pay me to perform more service and better service than what I was actually paid to perform. This idea has become a fixed principle with me, and it now modifies all of the actions I take to render service.

In Business College I rubbed elbows with young men and young women who, like me, were there for only one purpose, and that was to learn to render efficient service and earn a living. I met Jew and Gentile, Catholic and Protestant, all on exactly the same terms, and learned for the first time that all were human and all responded to that simple spirit of democracy that prevailed in the business college environment.

After finishing my business college training, I secured a position as stenographer and bookkeeper, and worked in this capacity for the ensuing five years. As a result of this idea of performing more service and better service than paid for, which I had learned in business college, I advanced rapidly and always succeeded in filling positions of responsibility far in advance of my years, with salary proportionate.

I saved money and soon had a bank account amounting to thousands of dollars. I was rapidly advancing toward my rainbow's end. I aimed to succeed, and my idea of success was the same as what dominates the average youth's mind today—namely, money! I saw my bank account growing bigger and bigger. I saw myself advancing in position and earning more and more salary. My method of rendering service greater in quality and quantity than that for which I was paid was so unusual that it attracted attention and I profited by contrast with those who had not learned that secret.

My reputation spread rapidly and I found competitive bidders for my services. I was in demand, not because of what I knew, which was little enough, but because of my willingness to make the best use of what little I did know. This spirit of willingness proved to be the most powerful and strategic principle I ever learned.

SECOND TURNING POINT

The tides of fate blew me southward and I became the sales manager for a large lumber manufacturing concern. I knew nothing about lumber and I knew nothing about sales management, but I had learned that it paid to render better service and more of it than I was paid for, and with this principle as the dominating spirit, I tackled my new job with the determination to find out all I could about selling lumber.

I made a good record. My salary was increased twice during the year, and my bank account continued growing bigger and bigger. I did so well in managing the sales of my employer's lumber that he organized a new lumber company and took me into partnership with him as a half-owner in the business.

The lumber business was good and we prospered.

I could see myself drawing nearer and nearer to the rainbow's end. Money and success poured in on me from every direction, all of which fixed my attention steadfastly on the pot of gold that I could plainly see just ahead of me. Up to this time it had never occurred to me that success could consist of anything except gold! Money in the bank represented the last word in attainment. Being of that breezy, good-fellow type. I made friends rapidly in the lumber circles and soon developed into a front-row man at the lumber conventions and at gatherings of lumbermen.

I was succeeding rapidly and I knew it!

Above everything else, I knew I was engaged in exactly the business I was best suited for. Nothing could have induced me to change my business. That is, nothing except for what happened.

The unseen hand allowed me to strut around under the influence of my vanity until I had commenced to feel my importance. In the light of more sober years and more accurate interpretation of human events, I now wonder if the unseen hand does not purposely permit us foolish human beings to parade before our own mirror of vanity until we come to see how vulgar we are acting and quit it. At any rate, I seemed to have a clear track ahead. There was coal in the furnace and water in the tank. My hand was on the throttle and I opened it wide.

Fate was awaiting me just around the bend with a stuffed club, and it was not stuffed with cotton, but of course I did not see the impending crash until it came. Mine was a sad story, but not unlike what many another might tell if he would be frank with himself.

Like a stroke of lightning out of a clear sky, the 1907 panic swept down on me. Overnight it swept away every dollar I had. The man with whom I was in business withdrew, panic-stricken but without loss, and left me with nothing but the empty shell of a company that owned nothing except a good reputation. I could have bought a hundred thousand dollars' worth of lumber on that reputation. A crooked lawyer (who afterward served a term in the penitentiary for some other offense, the details of which are too numerous to be enumerated) saw a chance to cash the reputation and what was left of the lumber company that had been left in my hands. He and a group of other men purchased the company and continued to operate it.

I learned a year later that they bought every dollar's worth of lumber they could get hold of, resold it, and pocketed the proceeds without paying for it; thus I had been the innocent means of helping them defraud their creditors, who learned after it was too late that I was in no way connected with the company.

That failure, while it worked a hardship on those who suffered loss as a result of my reputation having been wrongly used, proved to be the second important turning point in my life, because it forced me out of a business that offered no possibility of any remuneration except money, and no opportunity for personal growth from "within."

I fought with all my might and main to save my company during the panic, but I was as helpless as a suckling babe, and the swirl carried me out of the lumber business and into a law school, where I succeeded in rubbing off some more of my ignorance, vanity, and illiteracy, a trio against which no man can successfully compete.

THIRD TURNING POINT

It required the 1907 panic and the failure that it brought me to divert and redirect my efforts from the lumber business to the study of law. Nothing on earth except failure—or what I then called failure—could have brought about this result. Thus the second important turning point of my life was ushered in on the wings of failure, which reminds me to say that there is a great lesson in every failure, whether we learn what it is or not.

When I entered law school it was with the firm belief that I would emerge doubly prepared to catch up with the end of the rainbow and claim my pot of gold. I still had no higher aspiration than that of accumulating money, yet the very thing that I worshipped most seemed to be the most elusive thing on earth, for it was always evading me—always in sight but always just out of reach.

I attended law school at night and worked as an automobile salesman during the day. My sales experience in the lumber business was turned to good advantage. I prospered rapidly, doing so well (and still featuring the habit of performing more service and better service than paid for) that the opportunity came to enter the automobile manufacturing business. I saw the need for automobile mechanics, therefore I opened an educational department and began to train ordinary machinists in automobile assembling and repair work. This school prospered until it was paying me a great deal of money monthly in net profits.

Again I saw my rainbow's end in sight. Again I knew I had at last found my niche in the world's work. Again I knew that nothing could swerve me from my course or cause me to divert my attention from the automobile business. My banker saw me prospering. He extended me credit for expansion. He encouraged me to invest in outside lines of business. My banker was one of the finest men in the world, so he appeared to me. He loaned me many thousands of dollars on my own signature, without endorsement.

But, alas! It were ever thus—the sweet usually precedes the bitter. My banker loaned me money until I was hopelessly in his debt, then he took over my business. It all happened so suddenly that it dazed me. I didn't think such a thing possible. You see, I had still to learn much about the ways of men, especially the type who, unfortunately, my banker turned out to be—a type which, in justice to the business of banking, I ought to say is rarely found in that business.

From a man of affairs with a huge net income, owner of half a dozen expensive automobiles and much other junk that I didn't need but didn't know it, I was suddenly reduced to poverty.

The rainbow's end disappeared, and it was many years afterward before I learned that this failure was probably the greatest single blessing that ever was showered upon me, because it forced me out of a business that in no way helped to develop the human side, and diverted my efforts into a channel that brought me a rich experience that I greatly needed.

I believe it worthy of note to here state that I went back to Washington, D.C., a few years after this event and, out of curiosity, visited the old bank where I once had a liberal line of credit—expecting, of course, to find a prosperous bank still in operation.

To my great dismay, I found that the bank had gone out of business, the banking house was being used as a lunchroom for workmen, and my erstwhile banker friend had been reduced to penury and want. I met him on the street, practically penniless. With eyes red and swollen, he aroused in me a questioning attitude, and I wondered, for the first time in my life, if one might find any other thing of value, except money, at the rainbow's end.

Mind you, this temporary questioning attitude was not an open rebellion, nor did I pursue it far enough to get the answer. It merely came as a fleeting thought and passed out of my mind. Had I known as much then about interpreting human events as I now know, I would have recognized this circumstance as a nudge the unseen hand was giving me. Had I known anything about the law of compensation, I would not have been surprised when I found my banker reduced to poverty, knowing, as I did after it was too late, that my experience was but one of hundreds of similar ones that marked his code of business ethics.

I never put up. a stronger battle in my life than I did in trying to remain in the automobile business. I borrowed heavily from my wife and sunk it in a vain effort to remain in what I believed to be the business for which I was best fitted. But forces over which I had no control, and which I did not understand at that time, would have none of my efforts to remain in the automobile business. It was at a heavy cost of pride that I finally submitted, and turned, for want of knowing what else to do, to using the knowledge of law that I had acquired.

FOURTH TURNING POINT

Because I was my wife's husband and her people had influence; I secured an appointment as assistant to the chief counsel for one of the largest corporations of its kind in the world. My salary was greatly out of proportion to what the company had usually paid beginners, and still further out of proportion to what I was worth, but pull was pull, and I was there because I was there. It turned out that what I lacked in legal ability I supplied through that one sound fundamental principle I had learned in Business College—namely, to render more service and better service than paid for, wherever possible.

I was holding my position without difficulty. I practically had a berth for life if I cared to keep it. One day I did what my close personal friends and relatives said was a very foolish thing. I quit my job abruptly. When pressed for a reason, I gave what seemed to me to be a very sound one, but I had trouble convincing the family circle that I had acted wisely, and still greater difficulty convincing a few of my friends that I was perfectly rational in mind.

I quit that position because I found the work too easy and I was performing it with too little effort. I saw myself drifting into the habit of inertia. I felt myself loving to take things easily and knew that the next step would be retrogression. There was no particular impelling urge that forced or induced me to keep moving. I was among friends and relatives. I had a job that I could keep as long as I wished it, at a salary that provided a home, a good car, and enough gasoline to run it.

What else did I need? This was the attitude toward which I felt myself slipping. It was an attitude that startled me. However ignorant I might have been in other matters at that time, I have always felt thankful for having had enough sense to realize that strength and growth come only from struggle, that disuse brings atrophy and decay.

This move proved to be the next most important turning point in my life, although it was followed by ten years of effort that brought almost every grief the human heart could experience. I quit my job in the legal field, where I was getting along well, living among friends and relatives, with what they believed to be a bright and unusually promising future ahead of me. I am frank to admit that it has always been a source of wonderment to me as to why and how I gathered the courage to make the move that I did. As far as I am able to correctly interpret, I arrived at my decision more in the nature of a "hunch," or as a prompting that I little understood, than I did by logical deduction.

I selected Chicago as a location because I believed it to be the most competitive field in the world, feeling that if I could come to Chicago and gain recognition along any legitimate line, I would prove to myself that I had material in me that might someday develop into real ability. That was a strange process of reasoning; at least it was an unusual process for me at that time, which reminds me to admit that we human beings often take credit for intelligence to which we are not entitled. I fear that we too often assume credit for wisdom and for the results of causes over which we have absolutely no control and for which we are in no way responsible.

This is a thought that runs like a golden cord throughout my analysis of the seven most important turning points of my life. While I do not mean to convey the impression that all of our acts are governed by causes beyond our control, I do strongly urge upon you the wisdom of studying and correctly interpreting the turning points in our lives—the points at which our efforts are diverted from one direction to another, in spite of all we can do. I offer you no theory or hypothesis to cover this strange anomaly, believing that you will find your answer through the interpretative power of your spirit.

I came to Chicago without so much as a letter of introduction. My aim was to sell myself on merit, or at least on what I suspected of being merit. I secured a position as advertising manager. I knew next to nothing about advertising, but my previous experience as a salesman came to my rescue, and my old friend—the habit of performing more service than paid for—gave me a fair balance on the credit side of the ledger.

The first year I earned far more than I expected!

I was "coming back" by leaps and bounds. Gradually the rainbow began to circle around me, and I saw, once more, the shining pot of gold almost within my reach. I believe it of significant importance to bear in mind that my standard of success was always measured in terms of dollars, and my rainbow's end promised nothing but a pot of gold. Up to this point, if the thought ever entered my mind that anything except a pot of gold might be found at the end of a rainbow, that thought was momentary and left only a slight impression.

All down the ages, history is full of evidence that a feast usually precedes a fall. I was having my feast but did not expect a fall to follow it. I suspect that no one ever does anticipate the fall until it comes, but come it will, unless one's fundamental guiding principles are sound.

FIFTH TURNING POINT

I made a good record as advertising manager. The president of the company was attracted by my work and later helped organize the famous nationwide Betsy Ross Candy Company.

I became its president, thus beginning the next most important turning point of my life.

The business began to expand, until we had a chain of stores in eighteen different cities. Again I saw my rainbow's end almost within reach. I knew that I had at last found the business in which I wanted to remain for life, yet when I frankly admit that our policy and our business was fashioned after that of another candy company—whose western manager was my personal friend and former business associate, and that his overwhelmingly large success was the main factor in causing me to enter the candy business—you will be able to anticipate the finish of our candy enterprise before I mention it.

Pardon me for digressing a moment while I philosophize on a point that has brought deserved defeat to millions of people—namely, the practice of appropriating another person's plan instead of working out a plan of one's own origin.

The public is never in sympathy with a person who is obviously copying someone else's plan, even though such practice is not prohibited legally.

Nor is the resentment of the public the most damaging factor one who makes this mistake must contend with; the practice seems to take away the enthusiasm a person usually puts into a plan that is conceived in his own heart and brought to maturity in his own brain.

Everything went smoothly for a time, until my business associate and a third man, whom we later brought into the business, took a notion to gain control of my interest without paying for it—a mistake that men never seem to understand they are making until it is too late and they have paid the price of their folly.

Their plan worked, but I balked more stiffly than they had anticipated. Therefore, to gently urge me along toward the "grand exit," they had me arrested on a false charge and offered to settle out of court if I would turn over my interest in the company. I refused and insisted on going to trial on the charge. When the time arrived, no one was present to prosecute. We insisted on prosecution and requested the court to summon the complaining witness and make him prosecute, which was done.

The judge stopped the proceedings and threw the case out of court before it had gone very far, with the statement that "This is one of the most flagrant cases of attempted coercion that has ever come before me."

To protect my character, I brought suit for damages. The case was tried five years later and I secured a heavy judgment in the superior court of Chicago. The suit was what is called a "tort action," meaning that it claimed damages for malicious injury to reputation. A judgment secured under a tort action carries with it the right to imprison the one against whom the judgment is secured until the judgment is paid.

But I suspect another and much more exacting law than that under which tort actions may be brought was operating during those five years, because one of the parties—in whose brain the plan to have me arrested hatched—was serving a term in the federal penitentiary for another unrelated crime before my action against him was tried. The other party had fallen from a high station in life to poverty and disgrace.

My judgment stands on the records of the superior court of Chicago as silent evidence of vindication of my character, as well as evidence of something even more important. It's evidence that the unseen hand guiding the destiny of truth-seekers had eliminated from my nature all desire for my "pound of flesh." My judgment was not collected, and never will be. At least I will never collect it, because I suspect it has been paid, many times over. It has been paid in blood and remorse and regret and failure visited upon those who would have destroyed my character for personal gain.

This incident was one of the greatest single blessings that ever came to me, because it taught me to forgive; it taught me, also, that the law of compensation is always and everywhere in operation, and that "Whatsoever a man soweth, that shall he also reap." It blotted out of my nature the last lingering thought of seeking personal revenge at any time and under any circumstances. It taught me that time is the friend of all who are right and the mortal enemy of all who are unjust and destructive. It brought me nearer to a full understanding of the Master when he said, "Forgive them, Father, for they know not what they do."

A strange thing has just happened!

A moment ago I took out my watch; it slipped from my hands and crashed to pieces on the floor. I picked up the dead remains of what was a splendid timepiece only a few moments ago, and as I turned it over and looked at it, I was reminded that nothing ever "just happens;" that my watch was created by a superior, to perform a definite work, according to a definite plan. How much more certain it is that we human beings were created by a superior, according to a definite plan, to perform a definite work.

What a blessing it is when we come into realization of the fact that probably we were not intended as destructive factors, and that everything we accumulate in the way of material wealth will finally become as useless as the dust to which our flesh and bones will return.

I sometimes wonder if a full realization of this truth does not come more easily to the person who has been sinned against and spat upon and slandered and crucified on the cross of ignorance. I sometimes wonder if it were not well for all of us to undergo these experiences that try our faith and exhaust our patience and cause us to lose control of ourselves and strike back, because in this way we learn the futility of hatred and envy and selfishness and the tendency to destroy or undermine the happiness of a fellow being.

We can sharpen our intellect through the experiences of others, but our emotions are vitalized and developed only through our own personal experiences. Therefore, we can profit from every experience that works upon our emotions, whether that experience brings joy or grief. A close search of the biographies of people of destiny discloses the fact that nearly every one of them was sorely tried in the mill of merciless experience before they arrived, which leads me to wonder if the unseen hand does not test our metal in various and sundry ways before placing serious responsibilities upon our shoulders.

My space is too limited to permit me to philosophize further at this point, but I commend the thought it has raised to your serious consideration, that you may work it out to your own conclusions.

Before mentioning the next important turning point of my life, may I call your attention to two interesting facts—namely, that each turning point carried me nearer and nearer my rainbow's end, and each one brought me some useful knowledge that later became a permanent part of my philosophy of life. As well, those who tried to destroy me met with the same fate they tried to mete out to me.

SIXTH TURNING POINT

We come now to the turning point that probably brought me nearer the rainbow's end than any of the others had, because it placed me in a position where I found it necessary to bring into use all the knowledge I had acquired up to that time concerning every subject with which I was familiar. It gave me opportunity for self-expression and for personal development such as rarely come to a man early in life.

This turning point came when, after having been forced out of the candy business, I turned my efforts toward teaching advertising and salesmanship.

Some wise philosopher has said that we never learn much until we begin trying to teach others. My experience as a teacher proved that this is true. My school prospered from the start. I had a resident school and a correspondence school through which I was teaching students in nearly every English-speaking country.

In spite of the ravages of war, my school was growing by leaps and bounds and I saw the end of my rainbow drawing nearer and nearer. I was so close to it that I could almost reach out and touch the pot of gold.

As a result of the record I was making and the recognition I was gaining, I attracted the attention of the head of a corporation who employed me for three weeks out of each month at a salary considerably more than the president of the United States receives.

In less than six months, largely as a result of a series of strokes of good luck, I built up one of the most efficient working forces in America and increased the assets of the company to where it was offered far more for its business than it was worth when I took hold of its affairs.

Candidly, had you been in my place, would you not have felt justified in saying that you had found your rainbow's end? Would you not have felt justified in saying that you had attained success?

I thought I had, but one of the rudest shocks of all was still awaiting me, due partly to the dishonesty of the head of the corporation for which I was working, but more directly, I suspect, to a deeper and more significant cause concerning what fate seemed to have decreed I should learn.

One hundred thousand dollars of my salary was conditional upon my remaining as the directing head of staff for a period of one year. But in less than half that time I began to see that I was pyramiding power and placing it in the hands of a man who was growing drunk on it. I began to see that ruin awaited him just around the corner. This discovery brought me much grief. Morally, I was responsible for several million dollars of capital that I had induced the American people to invest in this corporation, although legally I was in no way responsible.

I finally brought the matter to a head, delivering an ultimatum to the head of the corporation to safeguard the funds of the company under a board of financial control or else accept my resignation. He laughed at the suggestion, because he thought I would not break my contract and thereby lose a large sum of money. Perhaps I would not have done so, had it not been for the moral responsibility that I felt obliged to carry out in behalf of thousands of investors. I resigned, had the company placed in the hands of the receiver, and thereby protected it against the mismanagement of a money-mad young man—a bit of satisfaction that brought me much ridicule from my friends and cost me a great sum.

For the moment my rainbow's end seemed vague and somewhat distant. There were moments when I wondered myself what caused me to make a fool of myself and throw away a fortune just to protect those who never would even know that I had made a sacrifice for them.

It was during one of these reminiscent moments that I felt a bell ringing in the region of my heart. At least the ringing of a bell is as near as I can come to describing the sensation I experienced. With the ringing of this bell came a message—a clear, distinct, unmistakable message. It bade me stand by my decision and be thankful that I had the courage to render it as I did. Remember what I have said about this ringing bell, because I am coming back to the subject again.

Since that eventful moment I have felt the ringing of the bell many times. I have now come to understand what it means. I respond to it and the message that follows it guides me in the right direction. Perhaps you would not have called the ringing of the bell a message, but I know of no other terms in which to describe these, the strangest of my life's experiences.

At this point I commenced to experience something more than the ringing of a bell. I commenced to wonder if my rainbow's end had not been evading me all these years, leading me up one hillside of failure and down another, because I was looking for the wrong reward! Mind you, I just questioned myself on this point—that was all.

This brings me to the seventh and last important turning point in my life.

Before I proceed to describe this last turning point, I feel it my duty to say that nothing that has been described up to this point is, within itself, of any practical significance. The six turning points I have described, taken singly, meant absolutely nothing to me, and will mean nothing to you if they are analyzed separately. But take these events collectively and they form a foundation for the next and last turning point; they constitute the very best sort of evidence that we human beings are constantly undergoing evolutionary changes as a result of the varying experiences with which we meet, even though no single experience seems to convey a definite, usable lesson.

I feel impelled to dwell at length on the point that I am trying to make plain, because I am now at the point in my career at which people go down in defeat or rise to heights of attainment that startle the world, according to the manner in which they interpret past events and build plans that are based upon past experiences. If my story stopped where I am at this moment, it could not possibly mean anything to you, but there is another and more significant chapter yet to be written covering the seventh and last important turning point in my life.

Up to now I have presented nothing but a more or less disconnected series of events which, within themselves, mean nothing. I repeat this thought because I want you to get it. And while you are thinking about it, I want to remind you that it is necessary to take a retrospective view of life every so often with the object of gathering all the more or less mean-ingless events together and interpreting them in the light of trying to discover what has been learned from them.

These experiences and failures and disappointments and mistakes and turning points in life might go on and on with-out benefit, until the grim reaper arrives and claims his toll, unless we awake to the realization that there are lessons to be learned from every one of them, and unless we commence tabulating the results of what we learn from those experiences so we can make use of them without having to repeat them over and over.

SEVENTH TURNING POINT

In my climax I will tabulate the sum total of all that I learned from each of the seven important mileposts of my life, but first let me describe the seventh and last of these turning points. To do so, I must go back one year to that eventful day—November 11, 1918.

That was Armistice Day, as everyone knows. Like most other people, I became as drunk with enthusiasm and joy that day as any man ever did on wine. I was practically penniless, but I was happy to know that the slaughter was over and rea-son was about to spread its beneficent wings over the earth once more.

The war had swept away my school, from which my income would have sustained me, had our boys not been drafted for the war. I stood as far away from my rainbow's end as I did on that eventful day more than twenty years previously, when I stood at the drift mouth of a coal mine where I was employed as a laborer and thought of the statement that kindly old gentleman had made to me the night before.

I now realized that a yawning chasm stood between me and any accomplishment, other than that of laborer in the mines.

But I was happy again! Then that tramp thought entered my consciousness and again prompted me to ask myself if I had not been searching for the wrong sort of reward at my rainbow's end.

I sat down to write with nothing particular in mind. To my astonishment, my hands began to play a regular symphony upon the keys. I had never written so rapidly or so easily before. I did not think of what I was writing—I just wrote and wrote and kept on writing.

When I was through I had five pages of manuscript and, as near as I have been able to determine, that manuscript was written without any organized thought on my part. It was an editorial out of which my first magazine, *Hill's Golden Rule*, was born. I took this editorial to a wealthy man and read it to him. Before I had read the last line, he had promised to finance my magazine.

It was in this somewhat dramatic manner that a desire that had lain dormant in my mind for nearly twenty years began to express itself in reality. It was the same idea I had in mind when I made the statement that caused the old gentleman to lay his hand on my shoulder and make that fortunate remark, twenty years previously. The idea had as its foundation the thought that the Golden Rule ought to be the guiding spirit in all human relationships.

All my life I had wanted to become a newspaper editor. Back more than thirty years ago, when I was a very small boy,

I used to "kick" the press for my father, who published a small newspaper, and I grew to love the smell of printer's ink.

Perhaps this desire was subconsciously gaining momentum until it finally had to burst forth in terms of action. Or maybe there was another plan over which I had no control, and with the building of which I had nothing to do, that urged me on and on, never giving me a moment's rest in any other line of work until I began my first magazine. The point can be passed for the moment.

The important thing to which I would direct your attention is the fact that I found my proper niche in the world's work and I was very happy over it. Strangely enough, I entered into this work, which constituted my last lap in the long, long trail I had traveled in search of my rainbow's end, with never a thought of finding a pot of gold. For the first time in my life, I seemed to sense there was something else to be sought in life that was worth more than gold. Therefore, I went at my first editorial work with only one thought in mind—and I pause while you ponder over this thought— and that thought was to render the world the best service I was capable of.

The magazine prospered from the beginning. In less than six months, it was being read in every English-speaking country in the world. It brought me recognition from all parts of the world, which resulted in a public-speaking tour that I made in 1920, covering every large city in America. This tour was an education within itself, because it brought me into exceedingly close touch with people in all walks of life, in all parts of the country, and gave me an opportunity to study their needs, their desires, and their emotions.

Up to and including the sixth of the important turning points in my life, I had made about as many enemies as I had friends. Now a strange thing has happened. Beginning with my first editorial work, I commenced to make friends by the thousands; today, upwards of 100,000 people stand squarely behind me because they believe in me and my message.

What brought about this change? If you understand the law of attraction, you can answer this, because you know that like attracts like and that we will attract friends or foes according to the nature of the thoughts that dominate our minds. One cannot take a belligerent attitude toward life and expect others to take anything except the same attitude toward us. When I began to preach the Golden Rule in my first magazine, I began to live it as near as I could. There is a big difference between merely believing in the Golden Rule and actually practicing it in overt acts, a truth that I learned when I began my first magazine. This realization brought me abruptly into understanding of a principle that now permeates every thought that finds a permanent lodging place in my mind, and dominates every act I perform, and that thought is none other than the one laid down by the Master in his sermon on the mount when he admonished us to do unto others as we would have others do unto us.

During these past three years, since I have been sending out Golden Rule thought vibrations to hundreds of thousands of people, these thought waves have multiplied themselves in the rebound and have brought back to me floods of goodwill from those my message reached. "Whatsoever a man soweth, that shall he also reap."

I have been sowing the seeds of kindness; I have been planting constructive thoughts where destructive ones existed before. I have been helping people see the folly of fighting among themselves and the virtue of cooperative effort, until I have charged and vitalized my very soul with these as my dominating thoughts, and they, in turn, have constituted a magnet that has attracted back to me the cooperation and goodwill of thousands who were in harmony with these thoughts.

I was rapidly approaching my rainbow's end for the seventh and last time. Every avenue of failure seemed closed. My enemies had been slowly transformed into friends, and I was making new friends by the thousand. But there was a final test that I had to undergo.

The unseen hand does not disseminate its precious jewels of knowledge without a price, nor does it lift us into positions of responsibility or create people of destiny without testing their metal. This testing process usually takes place when we least expect it, thereby catching us off guard and giving us no chance to display anything except our real personalities.

When my testing time arrived it caught me unexpectedly and unprepared, due mainly, I suppose, to the fact that I had protected my flanks with nothing more than man-made appliances. I had relied too much on myself and not enough on the unseen hand. I had failed to strike a happy medium, where I maintained just enough but not too much self-reliance. Consequently, my last and most trying turning point brought me much grief, which I could have avoided had my knowledge of human events and of the power that controls human events been a little better balanced.

As I have stated, I was approaching the end of my rainbow with the firm belief that nothing on earth could stop me from attaining it and claiming my pot of gold and everything else that a successful searcher for this great reward might expect.

Like a stroke of lightning out of a clear sky, I received a shock!

The "impossible" had happened. My first magazine, *Hill's Golden Rule,* was not only snatched out of my hands overnight, but its influence was temporarily turned as a weapon to defeat me.

Again people had failed me, and I thought unkind thoughts about them. It was a savage blow to me when I awoke to the realization that there was no truth to the Golden Rule—which I had been not only preaching to thousands of people, through the pages of my magazine and in person to hundreds of thousands, but had been doing my level best to live as well.

This was the supreme moment of test! Had my experience proved my most beloved principles to be false and nothing more than a snare with which to trip the untutored, or was I about to learn a great lesson that would establish the truth and the soundness of those principles for the remainder of my natural life and perhaps throughout eternity?

These were the questions that passed through my mind.

I did not answer them quickly. I could not. I was so stunned that I simply had to stop and catch my breath. I had been preaching that one could not steal another man's idea or his plans or his goods and wares and still prosper. My experience seemed to give the lie to all I had ever written or spoken along this line, because those who stole the child of my heart and brain seemed not only to be prospering with it, but they had actually used it as a means of stopping me from carrying out my plans for worldwide service in the interest of the race.

Months passed by and I was unable to turn a wheel.

I had been deposed, my magazine had been taken away from me, and my friends seemed to look upon me as a sort of fallen hero. Some said I would come back stronger and bigger for the experience. Others said I was through. Thus the remarks came and went, but I stood looking on in wonderment, feeling much the same as a person feels who is undergoing a nightmare and knows what is going on around him but is unable to awake or move as much as a little finger.

Literally I was experiencing a wide-awake nightmare that seemed to hold me firmly within its grasp. My courage was gone. My faith in humanity all but gone. My love for humanity was weakening. Slowly but surely I was reversing my opinion concerning the highest and best ideals I had been building for more than a score of years. The passing weeks seemed like an eternity. The days seemed like a whole lifetime.

One day the atmosphere began to clear away.

And I am reminded to digress while I say that such atmospheres usually do clear away. Time is a wonderful healer of wounds. Time cures nearly everything that is sick or ignorant, and most of us are both at times.

During the seventh and last turning point in my life, I was reduced to greater poverty than any I had ever known before. From a well-furnished home I was reduced, practically overnight, to a one-room apartment. Coming, as this blow did, just as I was about to lay hold of the pot of gold at my rainbow's end, it cut a deep and ugly wound in my heart. During this brief testing spell I was made to kneel in the very dust of poverty and eat the crusts of all my past follies. When I had all but given up, the clouds of darkness began to float away as rapidly as they had covered me.

I stood face to face with one of the most trying tests that ever came to me. Perhaps no human being was more severely tried than I was. At least that was the way I felt about it at the time.

The postman had delivered my scant collection of mail. As I opened it I was watching the pale red sun as it had all but disappeared over the western horizon. To me it was symbolic of what was about the happen to me, for I saw my sun of hope also setting in the West.

I slit open the envelope on top, and as I did so a certificate of deposit fluttered to the floor and fell face upward. It was for $25,000. For a whole minute I stood with my eyes glued to that bit of paper, wondering if I were dreaming. I walked over closer to it, picked it up, and read the letter accompanying it.

That money was all mine! I could draw it out of the bank at will. Only two slight strings were tied to it, but they made it necessary for me to obligate myself, morally, to turn my back on everything I had been preaching, about placing the interests of the people above those of any individual.

The supreme moment of test had come.

Would I accept that money, which was ample capital with which to publish my magazine, or would I return it and carry on a little longer? Those were the first questions that claimed my attention.

Then I heard the ringing of the bell in the region of my heart. This time its sound was more direct. It caused the blood to tingle through my body. With the ringing of the bell came the most direct command that ever registered itself in my consciousness, and it was accompanied by a chemical change in my brain such as I had never experienced before. It was a positive, startling command, and it brought a message that I could not misunderstand.

Without promise of reward, it bade me return that $25,000.

I hesitated. The bell kept on ringing. My feet seemed glued to the spot. I could not move out of my tracks. Then I reached my decision. I decided to heed that prompting, which no one but a fool could have mistaken.

The instant I reached this conclusion I looked, and in the approaching twilight I saw the rainbow's end. I had at last caught up with it. I saw no pot of gold, except the one I was about to send back to the source from which it came, but I found something more precious than all the gold in the world as I heard a voice that reached me not through my ears but through my heart, and it said:

"Standeth God Within the Shadows of Every Failure."

The end of my rainbow brought me the triumph of principle over gold. It gave me a closer communion with the great unseen forces of this universe, and new determination to plant the seed of the Golden Rule philosophy in the hearts of millions of other weary travelers who are seeking the end of their rainbow.

Did it pay to return that $25,000? Well, I leave that to my readers to decide. Personally, I am well satisfied with my decision, following which a strange and unexpected thing happened: all the capital I needed came not from one source alone but from many sources. It came in abundance, without any chain of gold tied to it or any embarrassing conditions placed upon it that sought to control my pen.

In an earlier issue of this magazine, my secretary tells of one of the most dramatic events that followed closely upon my decision not to accept financial help from sources that would, to any extent whatsoever control my pen. That incident is only one, each constituting sufficient evidence to convince all but fools that the Golden Rule really works, the law of compensation is still in operation, and "Whatsoever a man soweth, that shall he also reap."

Not alone did I get all the capital necessary to carry this magazine over the beginning period, during which its own revenues were insufficient to publish it, but what is of far greater significance, the magazine is growing with rapidity heretofore unknown in the field of similar periodicals. The readers and the public generally have caught the spirit behind the work we are doing, and they have put the law of increasing returns into operation in our favor.

Am I entitled to any credit for the events herein mentioned, some of which would seem to reflect credit upon me? Am I entitled to credit for the success that is now crowning the efforts I am exerting through the pages of this magazine?

Frankly, I feel impelled to answer in the negative!

I have been nothing more than a tool in the hands of a higher power, and I have played about the same part that a violin plays in the hands of a master. If I have struck a symphonic rhythm in the song I am trying to sing through the pages of this, the people's monthly messenger, it has been because I have resigned myself to the influence of the unseen hand. What I am trying to say is that I take no credit unto myself for anything of a creditable nature that I have done or may do. Had I followed what seemed to be my natural tendency and inclinations, I would have gone down to defeat at any one of the seven turning points in my life, but always there was a guiding force that came to my rescue and saved me from defeat.

I make these admissions in a spirit of frankness and with the earnest desire to help others benefit by my experiences, as herein set down. Many of my conclusions, you will of course realize, are purely hypothetical, yet I would feel myself to be a fraud of the first rank if I took unto myself, either by direct statement or by innuendo, credit for those higher impulses that actually had to break down my own natural tendencies in order to get a foothold on me. Had I followed my intellectual conclusions and tendencies, I would have gone down in defeat at every one of those seven turning points in my life, a conclusion that I am forced to reach in the light of a reasonably sound interpretation of the meaning of the lessons that each of these turning points taught me.

Now let me summarize the most important lessons that I learned in my search for the rainbow's end. I will not try to mention all the lessons, only the more important ones. I will leave to your own imagination much that you can see without my recounting it here.

First, and most important of all, in my search for the rainbow's end I found God in a very concrete, unmistakable, and satisfying manifestation, which is quite sufficient if I had found nothing more. All my life I had been somewhat unsettled in my own mind as to the exact nature of that unseen hand that directs the affairs of the universe, but my seven turning points on the rainbow trail of life brought me, at last, to a conclusion that satisfies. Whether my conclusion is right or wrong is not of much importance; the main thing is that it satisfies me.

The lessons of lesser importance that I learned are these:

I learned that those whom we consider our enemies are, in reality, our friends. In the light of all that has happened, I would not begin to go back and undo a single one of those trying experiences, because each one of them brought me positive evidence of the soundness of the Golden Rule and the existence of the law of compensation through which we claim our rewards for virtue and pay the penalties for our ignorance.

I learned that time is the friend of all who base their thoughts and actions on truth and justice, and that it is the mortal enemy of all who fail to do so, even though the penalty or the reward is often slow in arriving where it is due.

I learned that the only pot of gold worth striving for is that which comes from the satisfaction of knowing that one's efforts are bringing happiness to others.

One by one, I have seen those who were unjust and who tried to destroy me cut down by failure. I have lived to see every one of them reduced to failure far beyond anything that they planned for me. The banker whom I mentioned was reduced to poverty. The men who stole my interest in the Betsy Ross Candy Company and tried to destroy my reputation have come down to what looks to be permanent failure, one of them being a convict in the federal prison.

The man who defrauded me out of my $100,000 salary, and whom I elevated to wealth and influence, has been reduced to poverty and want. At every turn of the road that led, finally, to my rainbow's end, I saw indisputable evidence to back the

Golden Rule philosophy that I am now sending forth, through organized effort, to hundreds of thousands of people.

Last, I have learned to listen for the ringing of the bell that guides me when I come to the crossroads of doubt and hesitancy. I have learned to tap a heretofore unknown source from which I get my promptings when I wish to know which way to turn and what to do. These promptings have never led me in the wrong direction and I am confident they never will.

As I finish these lines, I see on the walls of my study the pictures of great men whose characters I have tried to emulate. Among them is that of the immortal Lincoln, from whose rugged, care-worn face I seem to see a smile emerging and from whose lips I can all but hear those magic words, "With charity for all and malice toward none." And deep down in my heart I hear the mysterious bell ringing, and following it comes, once more, as I close these lines, the greatest message that ever reached my consciousness:

"Standeth God Within the Shadow of Every Failure."

SIX

How Self-Confidence Lifted A Man In Four Days

The scientific principles outlined in this lesson have brought success and happiness to millions of people. The lesson you are about to read has an interesting history. I have evidence of more than a hundred cases of men and women finding their proper bearings in life in this way.

The most striking example of immediate transformation of failure into success, through the aid of this article, happened about four years ago. One day a homeless man came to my office. When I looked up at him, he was standing in the door with his cap in his hands, looking as if he wanted to apologize for being on earth.

I was about to offer him some change when he startled me by pulling a little brown-covered booklet out of his pocket. It was a copy of *How to Build Self-Confidence*. He said, "It must have been the hand of fate that slipped this little booklet into my pocket yesterday afternoon. I was on my way to punch a hole in Lake Michigan when someone gave me this book. I read it. It caused me to stop and think, and now I am satisfied that, if you will, you can put me back on my feet again."

I looked him over again. He was about the worst-looking specimen of humanity I have ever seen. He wore a two weeks' growth of beard. His clothes were un-pressed and ragged. His shoes were run down at the heels. But, he had come to me for help that I could not refuse. I asked him to come in and sit down. Frankly, I had not the slightest idea that I could do anything for him, but I did not have the heart to tell him so.

I asked him to tell me his story, to tell me what brought him down to that station in life. He told me his story. Briefly, it was this: He once was a successful manufacturer up in the state of Michigan till his factory failed. It wiped out his savings and his business, and the blow broke his heart. It undermined his faith in himself, so he left his wife and children and so he took to the streets.

After I had heard this story, I thought of a plan for helping him. I said to him, "I have listened to your story with a great deal of interest, and I wish I could do something for you, but there is absolutely nothing that I can do."

I watched him for a few seconds. He turned white and looked as if he were about to faint. Then I said, "But there is a man in this building I will introduce you to, and that man can put you back on your feet in less than six months if you will rely upon him." He stopped me and said, "For God's sake, lead me to him." I took him out into my laboratory and stood him in front of what looked to be a curtain over a door. I reached over and pulled the curtain aside, and he stood face to face with the person I mentioned, as he looked himself squarely in the mirror.

I pointed my finger at the mirror and said, "There is the only person on earth who can help you, sir; and unless you sit down and become acquainted with the strength behind that personality, you might just as well go ahead and 'punch a hole in Lake Michigan' because you will be no good to yourself or to anyone else."

He walked over real close to the glass, rubbed his bewhiskered face, then stepped back, and tears began to trickle down his cheeks.

I led him to the elevator and sent him away, never expecting to see him again.

About four days later, I met him on the streets of Chicago. A complete transformation had taken place. He was walking at a rapid pace with his chin up in the air at a forty-five-degree angle. He was dressed from head to foot with new clothes. He looked like success, and he walked as if he felt like success. He saw me and came over and shook hands.

He said, "Mr. Hill, you have changed the whole course of my life. You have saved me from myself by introducing me to myself—to my real self—the one I did not know before—and one of these days, I am coming back to see you again. When I do, I am going to be a successful man. I am going to bring you a check. Your name will be filled in at the top, and my name will be filled in at the bottom. The amount will be left blank, for you to fill in, because you have marked the biggest turning point in my life."

He turned and disappeared in the crowded streets of Chicago. As I watched him go, I wondered if I would ever see him again. I wondered if he would really make good. I just wondered and wondered. It seemed almost like reading some tale from the Arabian Nights.

Which brings me to the end of my introductory remarks, and to an appropriate place to say that this man has come back to see me again. He made good. If I mentioned his name in these columns, you would recognize it immediately, because he has attained phenomenal success and placed himself at the head of a business that is known from coast to coast.

I am trying to get him to tell his own story in these columns that others may profit by his example. I hope I will succeed, because there are millions of others who have lost faith in the only person on this earthly plane who can do anything for them, just as this man had done, who might find themselves through his own story.

In the meantime, following is the article that brought about this unusual transformation in a man who had fallen to the lowest depths of despondency.

This can prove to be the most valuable article you ever read. It shows you how to apply the principles of auto-suggestion and concentration in developing the most necessary of all qualities for success, self-confidence.

There are two great objects for which all humanity seems to be striving. One is to attain happiness, and the other is to accumulate material wealth—money!

You will begin to see the importance of developing self-confidence when you stop to realize that neither of these two chief objects of life can be achieved without it.

Try as hard as you wish, you cannot be happy unless you believe in yourself! Work with all the strength at your command, and you cannot accumulate more than barely enough to live on, unless you believe in yourself!

The one and only person in the world whose efforts can make you supremely happy under all circumstances, and through whose labor you can accumulate all the material wealth that you can use legitimately, is yourself.

When you come into a full realization of this great truth, a new, vibrant feeling of inspiration will seize you, and you will become conscious of a tremendous amount of vitality and power you did not know that you possessed before.

You will accomplish more, because you will dare to undertake more! You will realize, possibly for the first time in your life, that you possess the ability to accomplish anything you wish to accomplish! You will realize how little your success in any undertaking will depend upon others and how much it will depend upon you.

We recommend that you purchase a copy of Emerson's *Essays* and read "Self-Reliance." It will fill you with new inspirations, enthusiasm, and determination.

Then, after you have read the essay on self-reliance, read the one on compensation. In these two essays, you will find some remarkably helpful truths.

In the development of self-confidence, one of the first steps you must take is to dispel forever the feeling that you cannot accomplish anything you undertake. Fear is the chief negative that stands between you and self-confidence, but we shall show you how to scientifically eliminate fear and develop courage in its place.

Reposing in your brain is a sleeping genius who can never be aroused except through the exercise of self-confidence.

When it is once aroused, you will be amazed at what you can accomplish. You will surprise all who knew you before your transformation took place. You will brush aside all obstacles and sweep on to victory, backed by an invisible force that recognizes no obstacles.

A careful analysis of the successful people of the world shows that the dominating quality they all possessed was self-confidence.

The purpose of this chart is to show you how you may, through the principles of auto-suggestion and concentration, place any thought or desire in your conscious mind and hold it there until it becomes crystallized into reality. These principles are scientific and accurate. They have been tested thousands of times by leading scientists of the world. To prove their accuracy, you have only to try them out, as hundreds of others are doing, by memorizing the following:

THE GREAT SELF-CONFIDENCE CHART

1. I know that I have the ability to accomplish all that I undertake. I know that to succeed, I have only to establish this belief in myself and follow it with vigorous, aggressive action. I will establish it.

2. I realize that my thoughts eventually reproduce themselves in material form and substance and become real in the physical state. Therefore, I will concentrate upon the daily task of thinking of the person I intend to be and of drawing a mental picture of this person and of transforming this picture into re-

ality. (Here describe in detail your "chief aim" or the life-work you have selected.)

3. I am studying with the firm intention of mastering the fundamental principles through which I may attract to me the desirable things of life. Through this study, I am becoming more self-reliant and more cheerful. I am developing more sympathy for my fellows, and I am becoming stronger, both mentally and physically. I am learning to smile the smile that plays upon the heart as well as upon the lips.

4. I am mastering and overpowering the habit of starting something that I do not finish. From this time forward, I will first plan all that I wish to do, making a clear mental picture of it, and then I will let nothing interfere with my plans until I have developed them into realities.

5. I have clearly mapped out and planned the work that I intend to follow for the ensuing five years. I have set a price upon my services for each of the five years, a price that I intend to command through strict application of the principle of efficient, satisfactory service!

6. I fully realize that genuine success will come only through strict application of the "Golden Rule" principles. I will, therefore, engage in no transaction which does not benefit alike all who participate in it. I will succeed by attracting to me the forces that I wish to use. I will induce others to serve me because of my willingness to serve them. I will gain the friendship of my fellows because of my kindness and my willingness

to be a friend. I will eliminate fear from my mind by developing courage in its place. I will eliminate skepticism by developing faith. I will eliminate hatred and cynicism by developing love for humanity.

7. I will learn to stand upon my feet and express myself in clear, concise, and simple language, and to speak with force and enthusiasm, in a matter that will carry conviction. I will cause others to become interested in me, because I will first become interested in them. I will eliminate selfishness and develop in its place the spirit of service.

Let us particularly direct your attention to the second paragraph of this self-confidence building chart. Under this heading, you must clearly and definitely state your "chief aim." By deliberately placing it in your conscious mind, you are making use of the principle of auto-suggestion. By memorizing this chart and holding its contents in readiness, you may call it into the conscious mind at any minute, and by actually calling it into your consciousness many times a day, you are making use of the principle of concentration.

Your mind may be likened to the sensitive plate of a camera. The "chief aim" held before your mind, through the foregoing chart, may be likened to the object you want to clearly picture. When this picture becomes transferred permanently to the sensitive plates of your subconscious mind, you will notice that every act and every movement of your body will have a tendency toward transforming this picture into a physical reality.

Your mind first draws a picture of what it wants, and then it proceeds to direct your bodily activity toward acquiring it.

Keep fear away from your conscious mind as you would keep poison out of your food, for it is the one barrier that will stand between you and self-confidence.

After you have committed this self-confidence building chart to memory, make a habit of repeating it aloud at least twice a day. All of your thoughts have a tendency to produce appropriate or corresponding activities in your body, but thoughts that are followed by affirmation through spoken words will crystallize into reality in much less time than those not followed by expression in words. Going still further, thoughts which are followed by both spoken and written words will crystallize into physical reality in still less time than those that are inhibited and merely held in consciousness silently. Therefore, we not only strongly recommend you memorize this self-confidence building chart, but we also suggest that you write it out and repeat it aloud at least twice a day for at least two weeks. By following these suggestions, you will have taken three decided steps toward realizing your goal:

First, you will have created it in thought.

Second, you will have caused this to produce bodily action tending toward its ultimate transformation into reality, through the muscular action of the vocal organs in speaking aloud.

Third, you will have caused this thought to actually begin the process of transformation into physical reality through the muscular action of your hand in writing it out on paper.

These three steps would complete your task in many lines of work, for example, in architecture. The architect first thinks, paints a clear picture of a building on the sensitive plates of his or her mind, then transfers this picture to paper by hand, and lo! the work is completed.

We recommend that you stand before a mirror, where you can see yourself as you repeat the words of the self-confidence building chart. Look yourself squarely in the eyes as though you were some other person, and talk with vehemence. If there is any feeling of lack of courage, shake your fist in the face of that person you see in the glass and arouse a feeling of reaction. Make that image want to say and do something.

Soon you will actually see the lines on your face begin to change, from an expression of weakness to one of strength. You will begin to see strength and beauty in that face that you never saw before, and this wonderful transformation will be quite as noticeable to others.

You need not follow the exact wording of the self-confidence building chart, but select words that more appropriately express your desire. As a matter of fact, you may write an entirely new chart if you prefer. The wording is immaterial as long as it dearly defines the picture you intend to transform into reality.

Look at this chart as being a blueprint or detailed description of the person you intend to be. Record in the blueprint every emotion you wish to feel, every act you wish to perform, and a clear description of yourself as you wish others to see you. Remember that this chart is your working plan, and that in time—a very short time at that—you are going to resemble this plan in every detail.

Let this chart become your daily prayer, if you are so inclined, and repeat it as such. If you believe in prayer you cannot doubt for one moment that your desires, as expressed through the chart, will be fully realized. Do you see what a remarkable position of strength you will be in by repeating this chart as a prayer? Do you see with wonderful clearness just what the added quality of faith will do toward quickly and surely transforming your affirmations into physical realities? Do you not see the great possibilities of this method of using the power of the Infinite for the achievement of your desires?

It makes no difference what your religion may be; this method of self-development in no way conflicts with it. People of all religions recognize prayer as the central power around which their creeds are built. If prayer has the endorsement of all religions, it must be worthy of use in the achievement of legitimate ends. Surely the development of self-confidence is a legitimate and worthy end.

We may not be able to explain the wonderful phenomenon of prayer, but that should not prevent us from making every possible legitimate use of it. To make use of it in the transformation of the written words of the chart into physical reality surely is a legitimate use, because the purpose of this chart is the development of humanity, the greatest and most wonderful handiwork of God.

What could be a more worthy purpose than that of freeing the human mind from the greatest of all curses, fear? And, what is the self-confidence building chart for except to eliminate fear and build courage in its place?

By making use of this chart in the manner indicated, do you not see how one is placed in the position of being compelled to develop self-confidence or else doubt the power of prayer and aspiration? Do you see what a powerful impetus is given to your undertaking by the added quality of faith that accompanies prayer?

You need not confine your chart to the development of self-confidence exclusively. Add to it any other quality that you wish to develop, happiness for example, and it will bring you what you order. To deny this is to deny the power of prayer itself.

You are now in possession of the great passkey that will unlock the door to whatever you wish yourself to be. Call this great key whatever you wish. Consider it in the light of a purely scientific force if you choose; or, look upon it as a Divine Power, belonging to the great mass of unknown phenomena which mankind has not yet fathomed. The result in either case will be the same, success.

If prayer is good for anything at all, surely it may be used as a medium through which to develop in the human mind the greatest of all blessings, happiness. You will never enjoy greater happiness than that which you will experience through the development of self-confidence. Through this method of self-confidence building, your Creator stands as sponsor for your success. Do you not see what a tremendous advantage you are giving yourself through this procedure? Do you not see how impossible it will be for you to fail? Do you not see how prayer itself becomes your chief ally?

Faith is the foundation upon which civilization rests. Nothing seems impossible when built upon faith as the cornerstone to your self-confidence building. Make use of it, and your building cannot fall. You will overcome all obstacles, and tear down all resistance in accomplishing your purposes, through this simple plan. Let no prejudices stand in the way of your using this plan. To doubt that it will bring you that which you desire is the equivalent of doubting prayer.

The great curse of the ages is fear or lack of self-confidence. With this evil removed, you will see yourself being rapidly transformed into a person of strength and initiative. You will see yourself breaking out of the ranks of that great mass we call followers, and moving up into the front row of that select few we call leaders. Leadership only comes through supreme belief in self, and you know how to develop that belief.

Remember this as my parting shot to you—*that you can be anything that you deeply and emotionally desire to be.* Find out what you desire most, and you have then and there laid the foundation for acquiring it. Strong, deeply seated desire is the beginning of all human achievement—it is the seed, the germ from which all our accomplishments spring.

Emotionalize or vitalize your whole being with any well-fixed, definite desire, and immediately your personality becomes a magnet that will attract to you the object of that desire.

To doubt is to remain in ignorance.

SEVEN

The Miraculous Art
of Auto-Suggestion

The term *auto-suggestion* simply means a self-suggestion one deliberately makes to oneself. James Allen, in his excellent little magazine, *As a Man Thinketh*, has given the world a fine lesson in auto-suggestion by having shown that we may literally make ourselves over through this process of self-suggestion.

This lesson, like James's magazine, is intended mainly as a means of stimulating men and women to the discovery and perception of the truth that "they themselves are makers of themselves," by virtue of the thoughts they choose and encourage; that mind is the master weaver, both of the inner garment of character and the outer garment of circumstance; and that as they have woven in ignorance, pain, and grief, they may now weave in enlightenment and happiness.

This lesson is not a preachment, nor is it a treatise on morality or ethics. It is a scientific treatise through which the student may understand the reason why the first rung in the magic ladder to success was placed there, and how to make the principle behind that rung a part of his or her own working equipment with which to master life's most important economic problems.

This lesson is based upon the following facts:

1. Every movement of the human body is controlled and directed by thought, that is, by orders sent out from the brain, where the mind has its seat of government.

2. The mind is divided into two sections, one called the conscious section (which directs our bodily activities while we are awake), and the other called the subconscious section, which controls our bodily activity while we are asleep.

3. The presence of any thought or idea in one's conscious mind (and probably the same is true of thoughts and ideas in the subconscious division of the mind) tends to produce an "associated feeling," urging one to the appropriate bodily activity that will transform the thought into physical reality. For example, one can develop courage and self-confidence by the use or the thought of the following or similar positive statement: "I believe in myself. I am courageous. I can accomplish whatever I undertake." This is called autosuggestion.

FIND YOUR IDEAL WORK AND WRITE ABOUT IT

We shall now proceed to give you the operating method of the first step in the magic ladder to success. To begin with, search diligently until you find the particular work to which you wish to devote your life, taking care to see that you select work that will profit all who are affected by your activities. After you have decided what your life work is to be, write out a clear statement about it and then commit it to memory.

Several times a day, and especially just before going to sleep at night, repeat the words of this written description of your life work, and affirm to yourself that you are attracting to you the necessary forces, people, and material things with which to attain the object of your life work, or your definite aim in life.

Bear in mind that your brain is literally a magnet, and that it will attract to you other people who harmonize, in thought and in ideals, with those thoughts dominating your mind and those ideals most deeply seated in you.

HOW THE LAW OF ATTRACTION WORKS

There is a law, which we may properly call the law of attraction. It's this law that causes water to seek its own level, and everything throughout the universe of like nature to seek its kind. If it were not for this law, which is as immutable as the law of gravitation keeping the planets in their proper places, the cells from which an oak tree grows might scamper away and become mixed with the cells creating the poplar, thereby producing a tree that would be part poplar and part oak. But such a phenomenon has never been heard of.

Following this law of attraction a little further, we can see how it works out among men and women. We know that successful, prosperous people seek the companionship of their own kind, while the down-and-outers seek their kind, and this happens just as naturally as water flows downhill.

Like attracts like, a fact that is indisputable.

Then, if it is true that we are constantly seeking the companionship of those whose ideals and thoughts harmonize with our own, can you not see the importance of so controlling and directing your thoughts and ideals that you will eventually develop exactly the kind of "magnet" in your brain that will serve as an attraction in drawing others to you?

If it is true that the very presence of any thought in your conscious mind has a tendency to arouse you to bodily, muscular activity that will correspond with the nature of the thought, can you not see the advantage of selecting, with care, the thoughts you allow your mind to dwell upon?

Read these lines carefully, and think over and digest the meaning they convey, because we are now laying the foundation for a scientific truth that constitutes the very foundation upon which all worthwhile human accomplishment is based. We are beginning, now, to build the roadway over which you will travel out of the wilderness of doubt, discouragement, uncertainty, and failure, and we want you to familiarize yourself with every inch of this road.

No one knows what thought is, but every philosopher and everyone of scientific ability who has given any study to the subject is in accord with the statement that thought is a powerful form of energy that directs the activities of the human body, that every idea held in the mind through prolonged, concentrated thought takes on permanent form and continues to affect the bodily activities according to its nature, either consciously or unconsciously.

Auto-suggestion, which is nothing more or less than an idea held in the mind, through thought, is the only known principle through which one may literally make oneself over, after any chosen pattern.

HOW TO DEVELOP CHARACTER THROUGH AUTO-SUGGESTION

This brings us to an appropriate place to explain the method through which your author has literally made himself over during a period of approximately five years.

Before we go into these details, let us remind you of the common tendency of human beings to doubt what they do not understand, and cannot prove to their own satisfaction, either by similar experiences of their own or by observation.

Let us also remind you that this is no age for a Doubting Thomas. Your author, while a comparatively young man, has nevertheless seen the birth of some of the world's greatest inventions, the uncovering, as it were, of some of the so-called "hidden secrets" of nature. And he is well within the bounds of accuracy when he reminds you that science has lifted the curtains that separated us from the light of truth, and brought into use more tools of culture, development, and progress than had been discovered in all the previous history of the human race.

Within comparatively recent years, we have seen the birth of the incandescent electric light, the typesetting machine, the printing press, the X-ray, the telephone, the automobile, the airplane, the submarine, the wireless telegraphy, and myriad other organized forces that serve mankind and tend to separate us from the animal instincts of the dark ages.

As these lines are being written, we are informed that Thomas A. Edison is at work on a contrivance he believes will enable the departed spirits of men to communicate with us here on earth, if such a thing is possible. And if the announcement should come from East Orange, New Jersey, tomorrow morning, that Edison has completed his machine and communicated with the spirits of the departed, this writer, for one, would not scoff at the statement. If we did not accept it as true until we had seen proof, we would at least hold an open mind on the subject, because we have witnessed enough of the "impossible" during the past thirty years to convince us that there is little that is strictly impossible when the human mind sets itself to a task with that grim determination that knows no defeat.

If modern history informs us correctly, the best railroad officials in the country scoffed at the idea that Westinghouse could stop a train by jamming air on the brakes, but those same officials lived to see a law passed in the New York legislature compelling railroad companies to use this "foolish contrivance," and if it had not been for that law, the present speed of railroad trains and the safety with which we may travel would not be possible.

"IMPOSSIBILITIES" OF THE PAST

We are reminded to state also that, had the illustrious Napoleon Bonaparte not scoffed at Robert Fulton's request for an interview, the French capital might be sitting on English soil today, and France might be the mistress over all of the British Empire. Fulton sent word to Napoleon that he had invented a steam engine that would carry a boat against the wind, but Napoleon, never having seen such a contrivance, sent back word that he had no time to fool with cranks, and, furthermore, ships could not sail against the wind because ships never had been sailed that way.

Well within the memory of your author, a bill was introduced in Congress asking for an appropriation with which to experiment with an airplane that Samuel Pierpont Langley had worked out, but the appropriation was promptly denied, and Professor Langley was scoffed at as being an impractical dreamer and a "crank." No one had ever seen a man fly a machine in the air, and no one believed it could be done.

But we are becoming a bit more liberal in our viewpoint concerning powers we do not understand; at least those of us who do not wish to become the laughingstock of later generations are.

We felt impelled to remind you of these "impossibilities" of the past which turned out to be realities, before taking you behind the curtains of our own life and displaying, for your benefit, certain principles which we have reason to believe will be hard for the uninitiated to accept until they have been tried out and proved sound.

We will now proceed to unfold to you the most astonishing and, we might well say, the most miraculous experience of our entire past, an experience which is related solely for the benefit of those who are earnestly seeking ways and means to develop in themselves those qualities constituting positive character.

When we first began to understand the principle of autosuggestion several years ago, we adopted a plan for making practical use of it in developing certain qualities we admired in certain familiar characters in history.

Just before going to sleep at night, we made it a practice to close our eyes and see, in our imagination (please get this clearly fixed in your mind—what we saw was deliberately placed in our mind as instructions, or as a direct command to our subconscious mind, and as a blueprint for it to build by, through our imagination, and was in no way attributed to anything occult or in the field of uncharted phenomena) a large counsel table standing on the floor in front of us.

We then pictured, in our imagination, certain figures seated around that table, from whose characters and lives we wished to appropriate certain qualities to be deliberately built into our own character, through the principle of autosuggestion.

For example, some of those we selected to take an imaginary place at the imaginary counsel table were Lincoln, Emerson, Socrates, Aristotle, Napoleon, Jefferson, the man from Galilee, and Henry Ward Beecher, the well-known English orator.

Our purpose was to impress our subconscious mind, through auto-suggestion, with the thought that we were developing certain qualities we admired most in each of these and in other great ones.

Night after night, for an hour or more at a time, we went through this imaginary meeting at the counsel table. As a matter of fact, we continue the practice to this day, adding a new character to the counsel table as often as we find someone from whom we wish to take certain qualities, through emulation.

THE DIFFERENT QUALITIES OF THE GREAT

From Lincoln, we wanted the qualities for which he was most noted—earnestness of purpose and a fair sense of justice toward all, both friends and foes alike. He represented an ideal that had for its object the uplift of the masses, the common people. He also had the courage to break precedents and to establish new ones when circumstances demanded it. All these qualities, which we had so much admired in Lincoln, we set out to develop in our own character while looking upon that imaginary counsel table, by actually commanding our subconscious mind to use the picture it saw as a plan to build from.

We wished to take from Napoleon the quality of dogged persistency; we wanted his strategic ability to turn adverse circumstances to good account; we wanted his self-confidence and his wonderful ability to inspire and lead; we wanted his ability to organize his own faculties and his fellow workers, because we knew that real power came only through intelligently organized and properly directed efforts.

From Emerson, we wanted that remarkably keen insight into the future for which he was noted. We wanted his ability to interpret nature's handwriting as it is manifested in flow-ing brooks, singing birds, laughing children, the blue skies, the starry heavens, the green grass, and the beautiful flowers. We wanted his ability to interpret human emotions, his ability to reason from cause to effect and, inversely, from effect back to cause.

We wanted Beecher's magnetic power to grip the hearts of an audience in public address, his ability to speak with force and conviction that moved an audience to laughter or to tears and made his listeners feel with him mirth and melody, sorrow, and good cheer.

As I saw those men sitting there before me, seated around the imaginary counsel table, I would direct my attention to each of them for a few minutes, saying to myself that I was developing those qualities which I aimed to appropriate from the character before me.

If you have tears of grief to shed for me, on account of my ignorance in going through this imaginary role of character building, get ready to shed them now. If you have words of condemnation to utter against my practice, utter them now. If you have a feeling of cynicism which seems to strive for expression in the nature of a scowling face, give expression to it now, because I am about to relate something which ought to, and probably will, cause you to stop, look, and reason!

MY ASTOUNDING SUCCESS WITH THIS METHOD

Up until the time that I began these imaginary counsel meetings, I had made many attempts at public speaking, all of which had been dismal failures. *But with the very first speech*

I attempted to deliver after a week of this practice, I so impressed my audience that I was invited back for another talk on the same subject, and from that day until the time of the writing of these lines, I have been constantly improving.

Last year, the demand for my services as a public speaker became so universal that I toured the greater portion of the United States, speaking before the leading clubs, civic organizations, schools, and specially arranged meetings.

In the city of Pittsburgh I delivered the "Magic Ladder to Success" before the Advertising Club. In my audience were some of the leading business leaders of the United States, officials from the Carnegie Steel Company, the H.J. Heinz Pickle Company, the Joseph Home Department Store, and other great industries of the city. These were analytical people who knew when they heard something that was sound. At the close of my address, they gave me what several members of the audience afterward told me was the greatest ovation ever given a speaker before that club. Shortly after my return from Pittsburgh, I received a medal from the Associated Advertising Clubs of the World, in memory of that event.

Please do not make the mistake of interpreting the foregoing as an outburst of egotism. I am giving you facts, names, and places, and I am doing this only for the purpose of showing you that the quality I so greatly admired in Henry Ward Beecher I had actually commenced to develop in myself. This quality was developed, around the imaginary counsel table, with my eyes shut, while looking at an imaginary figure of Mr. Beecher seated as a member of my imaginary board of counselors.

The principle through which I developed this ability was auto-suggestion. I filled my mind so full of the thought that I would equal, and even excel, Beecher before I stopped that no other result could have been the outcome.

Nor is this the end of my narrative—a narrative which, by the way, the hundreds of thousands who know me now, located in nearly every city, town, and hamlet throughout the United States, can corroborate! I began, immediately, to supplant intolerance with tolerance; I began to emulate the immortal Lincoln in those wonderful qualities of justice toward all, friend and foe alike. New power began to come, not alone to my spoken words, but to my pen as well, and I saw, as plainly as I could see the sun on a clear day, the steady development of that ability to express myself with force and conviction by the written word.

In speaking of this very point, not many months ago, Mr. Myers, an official of the Morris Packing Company of Chicago, made the remark that my editorials in *Hill's Golden Rule Magazine* reminded him very forcefully of the late Elbert Hubbard, whom I admire, and added that he had just stated to one of his associates a few days previously that I was not only big enough to fill Elbert Hubbard's shoes, but that I had already outgrown them.

Again, I remind you not to brush these facts aside lightly, or to charge them to egotism. If I write as well as Hubbard, it is because I have aspired to do so, first having deliberately made use of auto-suggestion to charge my mind with the aim and purpose of not only equaling him, but of excelling him if possible.

I am not unmindful of the fact that the display of egotism is an unpardonable weakness, in either a writer or a speaker, and no one more readily denounces such shallowness of mind than this writer. However, I must also remind you that it is not always a sign of egotism when a writer refers to his own personal experiences for the purpose of giving his readers authentic data on a given subject. Sometimes it requires courage to do so. In this particular case, I would refrain from the free use of the personal pronoun "I" that has so frequently crept into this narrative, were it not for the fact that to do so would take away much of the value of my work. I am relating these personal experiences solely because I know they are authentic, believing, as I do, that it is preferable to run the risk of being classed as egotistical rather than use a hypothetical illustration of the principle of auto-suggestion or write in the third person.

THE VALUE OF A DEFINITE AIM IN LIFE

Your author gives the same care and attention to the details of his definite aim in life as he would to the plans of a skyscraper if he contemplated building one. Your achievement in life will be no more definite than the plans you used to attain your objective.

A little more than a year and a half prior to the writing of these lines, I revised my written statement of my definite aim in life, changing the paragraph headed "Income" to incorporate the higher sum I will need to carry on the educational program I have outlined for my School of Business Economics.

Within less than six months from the day that I made this change in the wording of my definite aim in life, I was approached by the head of a corporation who offered me a business connection at a salary of $105,200 a year, the $5,200 being intended to cover my traveling expenses to and from the place of employment, which was a long distance from Chicago, leaving the amount agreed upon for the salary exactly the amount that I had indicated in my written statement of my definite aim.

I accepted this offer, and in less than five months, I had created an organization and other assets for the concern that employed me that were estimated to be worth over $20 million. I refrain from mentioning names only for the reason that I feel duty-bound to state that my employer found a loophole through which he defrauded me out of the $100,000 salary agreed upon.

There are two outstanding facts I want to call to your attention, namely:

First, I was offered exactly the amount I had set out in my definite aim as being the amount I intended to earn during the ensuing year.

Second, I actually earned the amount (and, in fact, many times more than earned it) even though I did not collect it.

Now, please go back to the wording of my declaration that I would "earn $100,000 a year" and ask yourself the question, "What would have been the difference, if any, had the declaration read, 'I will earn and RECEIVE $100,000 a year'?"

Frankly, I do not know whether it would have made any difference in results if I had so worded my definite aim. On the other hand, it might have made a great deal of difference.

Who is wise enough to either affirm or deny the statement that there is a law of the universe through which we attract to us what we believe we can attain through this same law; that we receive what we demand, providing the demand is possible of attainment and is based upon equity, justice, and a clearly defined plan.

I am convinced that it is impossible to defeat the purpose of a person who organizes his or her efforts. Out of such organization your author has attained, with astounding speed, the position in life to which he aspired, and he knows anyone else can do the same.

Service and sacrifice arc passwords to the very highest success.

In my public addresses during the past twelve months, I suppose I have stated it as my opinion, at least a thousand times, that the person who takes the time to build a definite plan that is sound and equitable, that benefits all it affects, and then develops the self-confidence to carry it through to completion cannot be defeated.

I have never been accused of being overly credulous or superstitious. I have never been impressed very much by so-called miracles, but I am compelled to admit that I have seen the working out, in my own evolution during the past twenty-odd years, certain principles that have produced seemingly miraculous results. I have watched the development and unfoldment of my own mind, and while I ordinarily am not very deeply impressed by any "miracle" whose cause I cannot trace, I must admit that much has happened in the development of my own mind that I cannot trace back to original cause.

This much I do know, however; I know that my outward bodily action invariably harmonizes with and corresponds to the nature of the thoughts that dominate my mind, the thoughts I permit to drift into my mind, or those which I deliberately place there with the intention of giving them domination over my bodily activities.

My own experience has proved conclusively that character need not be a matter of chance! Character can be built to order just the same as a house can be built to correspond to a set of previously drawn up plans. My own experience has proved conclusively that a man can rebuild his character in a remarkably short length of time, ranging all the way from a few weeks to a few years, depending upon the determination and the desire with which he goes at a task.

A few months before I began these lessons on applied psychology, I had an experience that gained considerable attention among the interested parties here in the city of Chicago. As I was getting off an elevator in the retail department of A.C. McClurg & Company (Chicago's largest book and stationery house), the elevator man allowed the elevator door to slip and catch me between the door and the wall of the elevator. Besides causing me great pain, the accident tore the sleeve of my coat, damaging it to what looked like beyond repair.

I reported the accident to the store manager, a Mr. Ryan, who very courteously informed me that I would be reimbursed for the damage done. After a time, the insurance company sent out its agent, looked my coat over, and paid me for the damage. After the settlement was made and all parties concerned were satisfied, I took the coat to my tailor, and he made such a neat repair that one could not tell where the coat was torn.

The tailor's bill was a fraction of what I had received from the insurance company.

I had money, then, that did not belong to me, yet the insurance company was satisfied, mainly, I suppose, because it got off by paying for less than half the cost of a new suit. A.C. McClurg & Company was satisfied because my damage had been made good by their insurance company, and the affair had cost them nothing.

But I was not satisfied!

There were many purposes for which I could use that money. Legally, it belonged to me, I was in possession of it, and there was no one to ever question my right to it or the means by which I acquired it.

Had the insurance company known that the suit could have been so neatly repaired, it probably would have demurred against paying such a large bill, but the question of how the repair would turn out was one that could not be determined in advance.

I argued with my conscience for that extra money, but it would not permit me to keep it, so I finally compromised by handing back half of the amount and keeping the other half, on the theory that I had lost considerable time in bringing about the adjustment, and also on the theory that the repair might show up the defective part of the garment later on. I had to stretch matters considerably in my own favor before I felt justified in keeping more than the actual cost of the repairs.

When I handed back the money, the representative of McClurg & Company suggested that I just keep the money and forget it, to which I replied, "That's just the trouble; I would like to keep it, but I couldn't *forget* it!"

There was a sound reason why I handed back that money. That reason had nothing to do with ethics or honesty. It had nothing to do with the rights of A.C. McClurg & Company or of the insurance company that was protecting McClurg & Company. In arriving at my decision to hand back the money, I never took into consideration either McClurg or the insurance company. They were entirely out of the transaction because they were satisfied. What I really took into consideration was my own character, knowing as I did that every transaction was influencing my moral fiber, and that character is nothing more or less than the sum total of one's habits and ethical conduct. I knew that I could no more afford to keep that money without first having earned the right to it than an apple merchant could afford to place a rotten apple in a barrel of sound ones prior to storing the barrel away for the winter.

I gave it back because I wanted to convince *myself* that no material could find its way into my character, with my knowledge, except that which I knew to be sound. I gave back the money because it offered a splendid opportunity for me to test myself and ascertain whether or not I possessed that brand of honesty that exists for the sake of expedience, or that deeper, nobler, and more worthy brand that prompts one to be honest in order to grow stronger and more able to render service.

I am convinced that if our plans are based upon sound economic principles; if they are fair and just to all they affect; and if we, ourselves, can throw behind those plans the dynamic force of character and belief in self that grows out of the transactions that can satisfied conscience, we will ride on to success, with and by the aid of a tremendous current of force no power on earth can stop, a force which few can correctly interpret or understand.

Power is organized knowledge, controlled and directed to ends that are based upon justice and equity to all who are affected. There are two classes of human power. One is attained through the organization of the individual faculties, and the other is attained through the organization of individuals who work harmoniously to a common end. There can be no power except through intelligently directed organization.

You cannot organize your individual faculties except through the use of the principle of auto-suggestion, for the simple reason that you cannot vitalize or give dynamic force to your faculties, your emotions, your intellect, your reasoning powers, or your bodily functions, without collecting all of these together, co-relating them, and working them into a plan.

No plan, great or small, can be developed in your mind except through the principle of auto-suggestion.

The mind resembles a rich garden spot in that it will grow a crop of outward, physical, bodily activity that corresponds exactly to the nature of the thoughts that dominate the mind, whether those thoughts are deliberately placed there and held until they take root and grow, or merely drift in as so many stragglers, taking up their abode without invitation.

There is no escape from the effects of one's dominating thoughts. There is no possibility of thinking of failure, poverty, and discouragement and at the same time enjoying success, wealth, and courage. You can choose whatever holds the attention of your mind; therefore, you can control the development of your character, which, in turn, helps to determine the character of people you will attract to you. Your own mind is the magnet which attracts your associates to you, the station in life you hold. Therefore, it is within your province to magnetize that mind only with thoughts that will attract the sort of people with whom you wish to associate and the station in life which you are willing to attain.

Auto-suggestion is the very foundation upon which and through which an attractive personality is built, for the reason that character grows to resemble the dominating thoughts that help in the mind, and these, in turn, control the action of the body.

When you make use of the principle of auto-suggestion, you are painting a picture or drawing a plan for your subconscious mind to work by. After you learn how to properly concentrate or fix your attention on this process of plan building, you can reach your subconscious mind instantly, and it will put your plans into action.

Beginners must repeat over and over again the outline of their plans before the subconscious mind will take over the plans and transform them into reality. Therefore, be not discouraged if you do not get results on the spur of the moment. Only those who have attained mastership can reach and direct their subconscious mind instantaneously.

In closing this lesson, let me remind you that behind this principle of auto-suggestion is one important thing you must not overlook, and that is strong, deeply seated, highly emotional desire. Desire is the very beginning of mind operation. You can create in the physical reality practically anything you can desire with deep, vitalized emotion.

Deep desire is the beginning of all human accomplishments. Auto-suggestion is merely the principle through which that desire is communicated to your subconscious mind. Probably you do not have to go outside of your own experience to prove that it is comparatively easy to acquire what one strongly desires.

Next time, we will take up the subject of suggestion and show how to use your dynamic, attractive personality after you have developed it through auto-suggestion. Suggestion is the very foundation of all successful salesmanship.

EIGHT

Suggestion: More Effective Than a Demand

In the previous lesson, we learned the meaning of auto-suggestion and the principles through which it may be used. Auto-suggestion means self-suggestion. We now come to our next principle of psychology, which is as follows:

Suggestion is a principle of psychology by which we may influence, direct, and control the minds of others. It is the chief principle used in advertising and salesmanship. It is the principle through which Mark Antony swayed the Roman mob in that wonderful speech, outlined in "The Psychology of Salesmanship" (by Napoleon Hill).

Suggestion differs from auto-suggestion in only one way—we use it to influence the minds of others, while we use auto-suggestion in influencing our own minds.

Suggestion is one of the most subtle and powerful principles of psychology. Science has proved that through the destructive use of this principle, life may be actually extinguished, while all manner of disease may be eliminated through its constructive use.

On numerous occasions, I have demonstrated the remarkable power of suggestion in the following manner, before my classes in applied psychology:

Taking a two-ounce bottle labeled "Oil of Peppermint," I make a brief explanation that I wish to demonstrate the power of smell. Then, holding the bottle in front of my class so all may see it, I explain that it contains oil of peppermint, and that a few drops of it poured on a handkerchief which I hold in my hand will penetrate the farthest end of the room in about forty seconds. I then uncork the bottle and pour a few drops on my handkerchief, at the same time making a face to indicate that the odor is too strong. I then request the members of the class to hold up their hands as soon as they get the first whiff of the odor of peppermint.

The hands begin to go up rapidly until, in some instances, seventy-five percent of the class has their hands up.

I then take the bottle, drink the contents slowly and complacently, and explain that it contained pure water! No one smelled any peppermint at all! It was an olfactory illusion, produced entirely through the principle of suggestion.

In the little town where I was raised there lived an old lady who constantly complained that she feared death from cancer. As long as I can remember, she nursed this belief, sure that every little imaginary ache or pain was the beginning of her long-expected cancer. I have seen her place her hand on her breast and say, "Oh, I am sure I have cancer growing here." She always placed her hand on her left breast, the spot where she believed the cancer would attack her.

As I write this lesson, news comes that this old lady has died of cancer on the left breast, in the very spot where she placed her hand as she complained of her fears!

If suggestion will actually turn healthy body cells into parasites out of which a cancer grows, can you not imagine what it will do in eliminating diseased body cells and replacing them with healthy ones?

If an audience of people can be made to smell oil of peppermint when a bottle of plain water is uncorked, through the principle of suggestion, can you not see what remarkable possibilities there are for constructively using this principle in every legitimate task you perform?

Some years ago, a criminal was condemned to death. Before his execution, an experiment was performed on him that conclusively proved that through the principle of suggestion, death could actually be produced. This criminal was brought to the guillotine, his head placed under the knife after he had been blindfolded, and a heavy board was dropped on his neck, producing a shock similar to that of the knife of the guillotine. Warm water was poured gently and allowed to trickle slowly down his neck, to imitate warm blood. In seven minutes, the doctors pronounced the criminal dead. His imagination, through the principle of suggestion, had actually turned the sharp-edged board into a guillotine blade and stopped his heart from beating.

Every single case of the healing of disease by practitioners of "mental healing" is accomplished through the principle of suggestion. We learn from good authority that many physicians are using fewer drugs and more mental suggestion in their practice. Two physicians who are members of my own family supplied me with the information that they use more "bread pills" than they did a few years ago. One of these physicians told me of a case in which one of his patients was relieved of a violent headache in a very few minutes by taking what the patient believed to be aspirin, but which was, in reality, a white flour tablet.

Hypnotism operates entirely through the principle of suggestion. Quite contrary to the general belief, a person cannot be hypnotized without his consent. The truth is that it is the subject's own mind and not the mind of the operator or hypnotist that produces the phenomenon which we call hypnotism.

All the operator can possibly do toward hypnotizing a person is to "neutralize" the subject's conscious mind and then place in his subconscious mind whatever suggestions are desired. By "neutralizing" the mind, we have reference to the performance of overcoming or rendering powerless the conscious mind of the subject. We will come back to this subject again, and explain some of the methods through which the conscious mind may be rendered impotent or inoperative, but first let us understand the method through which hypnotism is produced, as described in the words of a hypnotist, as follows:

"After talking sympathetically with subjects, sometimes for an hour or two, about the failing they wish removed, thoroughly acquainting myself with their dominant propensities or controlling thought, and, above all, securing their confidence, I ask them to assume a comfortable reclining position on a lounge, and then continue a soothing conversation, such as the following, with the goal of producing a monotonous impression on eye and ear.

"I wish you would look at this diamond (or select any convenient object in line of vision) in a dreamy, listless manner and a blank, expressionless stare, thinking of nothing, not concentrating your mind or focusing your eye upon it, but relaxing the ocular muscles so that the object has a confused outline. Don't look the way you'd normally look when you'd like to distinctly see a nearby object. Rather, look through the stone and past it, as you look at a dead tree standing between you and a distant view you are contemplating.

"Make no effort, for there is nothing you can do to encourage the state of mind we're after. Do not wonder what is going to happen, for nothing is going to happen. Do not be apprehensive, or suspicious, or distrustful. Do not desire that anything shall take place, nor watch to see what may occur—nor seek to analyze what is going on in your mind. You are as negative, lazy, and indifferent as you can be without trying to be.

"You are to expect the familiar signs of the approach of sleep, and they are all associated with the failure of the senses and the standstill of the brain—heavy eyelids, reluctant ears, muscles and skin indifferent to stimuli of temperature, humidity, penetrability, etc. Already that delightful sensation of 'drowsiness' weighs your eyelids down and steeps your senses in 'forgetfulness,' and you yield to the impulse as the curtains are dropped between you and the outside world of color and light.

"And your ear seeks to share in the rest of the senses. As darkness is the sleep of the eye, so is silence that of the ear; and your ear secures silence by deadening itself to sound impressions. The sound of my voice loses interest for you, and all energy and conflict seem to be receding into a mysterious remoteness. A grateful sense of surrender to some pleasing influence you cannot and would not resist descends upon you and enwraps your whole body in its welcome embrace, and you are physically happy. Refreshing sleep has come to you."

From the foregoing, you have clearly seen that the hypnotist's first task is to render impotent the conscious mind. (By "conscious mind," we mean that division of the mind that we use when we are awake.) After the conscious mind has been "neutralized" or rendered inoperative, partly or in whole, the hypnotist manipulates the subject through suggestions direct to the subject's subconscious mind. The subconscious mind does whatever it is told. It asks no questions, but acts upon the sense impressions reaching it through the five senses. Reason, operating through the conscious mind, stands a sentinel during the waking hours, guarding the gateways of sight, smell, taste, touch, and hearing, but the moment we go to sleep or become semi-conscious from any cause, this guard becomes inoperative.

There are varying degrees of hypnotism to which a person may be subjected through the principle of suggestion. The professional hypnotist, performing on the stage, usually gains complete control of the subjects' minds, causing them to engage in all sorts of undignified and inconsistent antics. There is a much slighter degree of hypnotism to which people may be subjected, and through which they may be controlled without the hypnotist's being conscious of the fact. It is to this more "invisible" or unnoticeable degree of hypnotism that we wish to direct your attention, because it is the degree most commonly practiced by the nonprofessionals on those they choose to control or influence.

Whether subjects are under complete hypnotic control or only partly influenced, there is one condition which must exist in their minds, and that is credulousness. The hypnotist, whether of the professional or nonprofessional type, must first place these subjects in a state of abnormal credulousness before directing or control their minds.

In other words, before any mind can be influenced through suggestion, it must first be "neutralized." This brings us back to the question of describing the methods through which the mind may be "neutralized."

In other words, we shall now show you how to make practical application of the principle of suggestion, first warning you, however, that it will bring you success or failure, happiness or woe, according to the use you make of it!

I can best describe what is meant by "neutralizing" the mind by relating a case that covers the meaning very concretely. A few years ago the police arrested a gang of notorious crooks who were operating "clairvoyant" or "fortune telling" parlors in the city of Chicago. The head of this chain of fake shops was a man by the name of Bertsche. The scheme was to meet superstitious, credulous people of means who came to these shops to have their fortunes told and, by a series of mind manipulations that I will describe, to defraud them out of their money.

The "seeress" or woman in charge of one of these fake fortune telling shops would learn the secrets of her patrons, the extent of their finances, of what their wealth consisted, and all other necessary data. Getting this information was a simple matter, since the business of the fortune telling shop is to advise people in matters of business, love, health, etc. Suitable victims were located in this manner and the information gathered and passed on to the head of the "clairvoyant trust," Mr. Bertsche.

At the most opportune time, the "seeress" would advise her victim to consult with some businessman who could be trusted to be free from the kinds of prejudices common to "scheming blood relations," at the same time saying that the victim would soon meet such a man. Sure enough, pretty soon Mr. Bertsche "happens" to be in the fake fortune telling shop consulting "Madam Seeress" on matters of investment and business in general, and, by "mere accident," the victim is introduced to him.

"He is a man of great wealth," so the victim is told in confidence by the "seeress." She further confides the information that he is a "bighearted" man who loves to help other people succeed in business. Mr. Bertsche is faultlessly dressed and looks the part of wealth and prosperity. He meets the victim, chats pleasantly, and hurries away to meet an important engagement with "Mr. Morganbilt."

The next time the victim comes to the fake fortune telling shop, he or she (they duped both sexes with equal success) will likely see Mr. Bertsche "just leaving to keep another appointment with rich Mr. Vandermorgan." He hurries right on out, apparently showing but little deference to the victim. This performance is repeated several times, until the victim gets over his or her "gun-shyness" and begins to feel that Mr. Bertsche is a busy man, and that he has little time to devote to others.

Finally, after the victim has been carried through the first degree of mind manipulation and made to feel that a dinner invitation from Mr. Bertsche would be a highly honored privilege, such an invitation will be extended. The victim will be escorted to the most exclusive club, or the finest café, and treated to a dinner that will cost more than a whole week's living expenses would ordinarily cost. The bill is paid by the host, Mr. Bertsche, who has been introduced as "Judge" somebody or other, and who apparently is rolling in money and running to get away from its accumulation.

In Mr. Bertsche's inside pocket is a card index showing in detail every weakness, every eccentricity, every peculiarity of the victim, who has been accurately analyzed and charged. If he is a dog fancier, that fact is ascertained and charged. If he loves horses, that, too, is known.

The game has commenced! If, for example, the victim likes horseback riding, the affable, rich, and well-kept Mr. Bertsche will see to it that one of his thoroughbreds is placed at the victim's disposal. If the victim likes automobiling, affable Mr. Bertsche's Packard will be waiting at the door ready to accommodate.

The form of entertainment will vary according to the tastes of the victim, and the expense of it is always borne by the now "trusted friend," Mr. Bertsche. This line of procedure is kept up until the victim's mind is completely neutralized! In other words, until the victim entirely ceases to feel suspicious of anything that may happen or anything that may be said or even suggested. The affable Mr. Bertsche has completely wormed himself into his victim's confidence, all this coming about by the merest "accidental meeting," of course. In some cases, Mr. Bertsche would "play his victim" for six months before reaching the opportune moment at which to strike, and often the cost of the entertainment and the "settings of the stage" would mount up into the hundreds and even into the thousands of dollars.

According to the reports of the cases that came to light, some of Bertsche's victims gave up as much as $50,000 by "investing" funds in worthless enterprises, upon his recommendation, or upon his "casual" remark that he had funds invested in such and such a proposition that were paying him handsome returns. On one occasion, he casually displayed a "dividend" check for $10,000 he had just received from an investment of only $20,000 in some fake corporation. Mind you, he was too clever to try to persuade his victims to invest in one of these fake enterprises—he knew human nature too well for that—he merely was a bit "careless" in letting information out now and then that the victim could easily pick up and make use of.

Suggestion is more effective than out-and-out demand or request.

Subtle suggestion is a wonderful power, and "wealthy" Mr. Bertsche knew exactly how to apply it. On one occasion, it is said that his victim, an old woman, became so credulous that she actually drew a large sum of money out of the bank, took it to Mr. Bertsche, and tried vainly to get him to take it and invest it for her. He turned her away, telling her that he had surplus money of his own which he would like to put to work, and there was no opening just at that time. The reason the affable Mr. Bertsche turned the lady away was that he was playing her for larger stakes. He knew how much money she had, and he intended to get it all, so the lady was agreeably surprised a few days later when Mr. Bertsche telephoned her that, through a very special friend of his, she "might possibly get the chance" to invest in a certain block of very valuable stock, provided that she could take the whole block. He couldn't guarantee that she could get it, but she might try. She did! Her money was reposing in Bertsche's inside pocket an hour afterward.

We have gone into these details to show you exactly what is meant by rendering the mind "neutral." All that is needed to neutralize the mind and prepare it to accept and act under any suggestion is extreme credulousness, or credulousness greater than that normally exercised by the subject. Obviously, there are thousands of ways of neutralizing a person's mind and preparing it to receive any seed we wish to plant there through suggestion. It is not necessary to try to enumerate them, because you can draw from your own experience all that you will need to give you a practical working knowledge of the principle and its method of application.

In some cases, it may require months to prepare a person's mind to receive what you wish to place there through suggestion. In other cases, a few minutes or even a few seconds may be sufficient. You may as well accept it as a positive fact, however, that you cannot influence the mind of a person who is antagonistic toward you, or who has not implicit faith and confidence in you. The very first step to be taken, therefore, whether you are preaching a sermon, selling merchandise, or pleading a case before a jury, is to gain the confidence of whomever you wish to influence.

Read that remarkable speech of Marc Antony at the burial of Caesar, in Shakespeare's works, and you will see how a hostile mob was completely disarmed by Marc Antony through the use of the very same principle that we are describing in this lesson.

Let us analyze the beginning of this wonderful speech, for herein may be found a lesson in applied psychology that is second to none. The mob has heard Brutus state his reason for killing Caesar and has been swayed by him. Marc Antony, Caesar's friend, now comes onstage to present his side of the case. The mob is against him to start with. Furthermore, it is expecting him to attack Brutus. But Marc Antony, the clever psychologist that he is, does nothing of the sort. Says he, "Friends, Romans, Countrymen, lend me your ears; I come to bury Caesar, not to praise him."

The mob had expected that he had come to praise his friend Caesar (which he had), but he had no notion of trying to do so until the minds of the mob had been neutralized and prepared to receive favorably that which he intended to say. Had the plan upon which Marc Antony's speech was built been reversed, and had he referred sneeringly to Brutus as being an "honorable" man in the beginning, he would likely have been assassinated by the mob.

One of the most able and successful lawyers I ever saw makes use of the same psychology that Marc Antony employed, in addressing a jury. I once heard him address a jury with words which led me to believe, for a few minutes, that he was either drunk or that he had suddenly lost his reason.

He began by extolling the virtues of his opponents, and apparently he was helping them establish their case against his own client. He began by saying, "Now, gentlemen of the jury, I do not wish to startle you, but there are many points in connection with this case that are against my client," and he proceeded to call attention to every one of them. (These points, of course, had been brought out by opposing counsel anyway.)

After he had gone along this line for a time, he suddenly stopped and, with deep dramatic effect, said, "But—that is what the other side says about this case. Now that we know what their contentions are, let us turn to the other side of the case." From that point on, this lawyer played upon the minds of that jury as a violinist would play upon the strings of his instrument, and within fifteen minutes he had half of them in tears. At the end of his speech, he dropped into his seat, apparently overcome with emotion. The jury filed out and, in less than half an hour, returned with a verdict for his client.

Had this lawyer started out by stating the weak side of his opponent's case and urging upon the jury the merits of his own case too soon, he would undoubtedly have suffered defeat. But, as I afterwards learned, this lawyer was a close student of Shakespeare. He made use of the Marc Antony psychology in nearly all of his cases, and it is said that he lost fewer cases than any other lawyer in the community in which he practiced.

This same principle is used by successful salespeople, who not only refrain from "knocking" their competitor, but actually go out of their way to speak highly of the competition. Nobody ought to consider themselves finished salespeople until they have mastered the Marc Antony psychology and learned how to apply it. This speech is one of the greatest lessons in salesmanship ever written. If a salesperson loses a sale, the chances are about ninety-nine to one that he or she lost it because of lack of proper preparation of the prospective buyer's mind, spending too much time trying to "close" the sale and not enough time "preparing" the buyer's mind, and trying to reach a climax too soon. The successful salesperson must prepare the buyer's mind to receive suggestions without either questioning or resisting them!

The human mind is an intricate affair. One of its characteristics is the fact that all impressions which reach the subconscious division are recorded in groups that harmonize and are apparently closely related. When one of these impressions is called into the conscious mind, there is a tendency to recall all of the others with it. For example, one single act or word that causes a feeling of doubt to arise in a person's mind is sufficient to call into his conscious mind all of his experiences that caused him to be doubtful. Through the law of association, all similar emotions, experiences, or sense impressions reaching the mind are recorded together, so that the recalling of one has a tendency to bring out the others.

Just as a small pebble will, when thrown into the water, start a chain of ripples that will rapidly multiply, the subconscious mind has a tendency to bring into consciousness all of the associated or closely related emotions or sense impressions it has stored when one of them is aroused. To arouse a feeling of doubt in a person's mind has a tendency to bring to the surface every doubt-building experience that person ever had. That is why successful salesmen endeavor to keep away from subjects that may arouse the buyer's "chain of doubt impressions." The able salesperson has long since learned that to "knock" a competitor may result in bringing to the buyer's conscious mind certain negative emotions that may make it impossible for the salesperson to "neutralize" his mind.

This principle applies to and controls every emotion and every sense impression that is lodged in the human mind. Take the feeling of fear, for example; the moment we permit one single emotion that is related to fear to reach the con- scious mind, it calls with it all of its unsavory relations. A feeling of courage cannot claim the attention of our conscious mind while a feeling of fear is there. One must supplant the other. They cannot become roommates, because they do not harmonize. Every thought held in the conscious mind has a tendency to draw to it every other harmonious or related thought. You see, therefore, that those feelings, thoughts, and emotions claiming the attention of the conscious mind are backed by a regular army of supporting soldiers who stand ready to aid them in their work.

Place in a the mind, through the principle of suggestion, the ambition to succeed in any undertaking, and you will see latent ability aroused and power automatically increased. Plant in a child's mind, through the principle of suggestion, the ambition to become a successful lawyer, doctor, engineer, or entrepreneur, and if you keep away all counter-influences, you will see that child reach the desired goal.

It is much easier to influence a child through suggestion than it is an adult, for the reason that in the mind of a child, there are not so many opposing influences to break down in the process of "neutralizing" the mind, and children are natu- rally more credulous than an older person.

In the principle of suggestion lies the great roadway to suc- cess in the fields of organization and management. The super- intendent, foreman, manager, or president of an organization who fails to understand and use this principle is depriving himself of the most powerful force when it comes to influence.

One of the most able and efficient managers I ever knew was a man who never criticized any of his staff. To the contrary, he constantly reminded them of how well they were doing! He made a practice of going among them, stopping here and there to lay a hand on someone's shoulder to compliment that employee on his improvements. It made no difference how poor a man's work was, this manager never reprimanded him. By constantly placing in the minds of his men, through the principle of suggestion, the thought that "they are improving," they caught the suggestion and were promptly and effectively influenced by it.

One day, this manager stopped by the workbench of a man whose record showed that his work was decreasing in quantity. The man was working on piecework. Laying his hand on this man's shoulder, he said, "Jim, I believe you are doing much better work than you were last week. You seem to be setting the other boys a lively pace. I'm glad to see this. Go to it, my boy, I'm with you to the end!"

This happened about one o'clock in the afternoon. That night, Jim's tally sheet showed that he had actually turned out twenty-five percent more work than he had done the day before!

If anyone doubts that wonders can be performed through the principle of suggestion, it is because he or she has not given enough time to the study of the principle to understand it.

Have you not noticed that the friendly, enthusiastic, "breezy," talkative, "hail fellow well met" type of person gets along better than the more sedate as a leader in any undertaking? Surely you must have noticed that the grouchy, sullen, non-communicative sort of person never succeeds in attracting people or in influencing them. The principle of suggestion is at work constantly, whether we are aware of it or not.

Through this principle, which is as immutable as the law of gravitation, we are constantly influencing those around us and causing them to absorb the spirit we radiate and to reflect this spirit in everything they do.

Surely you have noticed how one disgruntled person will cast a shadow of discontent over others. One agitator or troublemaker can disrupt a whole work force and soon render their services worthless. On the other hand, one cheerful, optimistic, loyal, and enthusiastic person will influence a whole organization and inoculate it with that spirit.

Whether we know it or not, we are constantly passing on to others our own emotions, feelings, and thoughts. In most instances, we are doing this unconsciously. In our next lesson, we shall show you how to make conscious use of this great principle of suggestion, through the law of retaliation.

In the next lesson, we shall show you how to "neutralize" the mind and how to get people to work in complete harmony with you, through application of the principle of suggestion.

In this lesson, you have learned something about one of the major principles of psychology, which is suggestion. You have learned that there are two steps to be taken in manipulating this principle, as follows:

First, you must "neutralize" the subject's mind before you can influence it through thoughts you wish to plant there, through suggestion.

Second, to "neutralize" a mind, you must produce in it a state of credulousness greater than that normally maintained by the subject.

Fortunate is the person who controls egotism and the desire for self-expression to the extent that he or she is willing to pass on ideas to others without insisting on reminding them as to the source of those ideas. The one who begins a statement with "As you of course know, Mr. Smith," instead of "Let me tell you something you do not know, Mr. Smith," knows how to make use of the principle of suggestion.

One of the cleverest and most able salesmen I ever knew was a man who rarely took credit for any information that he passed on to his prospective buyers. It was always, "As you of course already know, so and so." The very effort which some people make to impress us with their superior knowledge acts as a negative barrier that is hard to overcome in the process of rendering our minds "neutral." Instead of "neutralizing" our minds, such people antagonize us and make impossible the operation of the principle of suggestion in influencing us.

As a befitting climax for this lesson, I shall quote an article written by Dr. Henry R. Rose, entitled "The Mind Doctor at Work." This is the clearest elucidation on the subject of suggestion that I have ever seen, and fully substantiates all that I have discovered in my research on this subject.

This article constitutes the finest lesson on suggestion that I have ever seen:

"If my wife dies, I will not believe there is a God." His wife was ill of pneumonia. This is the way he greeted me when I reached his home. She had sent for me. The doctor had told her she could not recover. She had called her husband and two sons to her bedside and bidden them goodbye. Then he asked that I, her minister, be sent for. I found the husband in the front room sobbing and the sons doing their best to brace him up. I went in to see his wife. She was breathing with difficulty, and the nurse told me she was very low. I soon found that Mrs. N had sent for me to look after her two sons after she was gone. Then I said to her, "You mustn't give up. You are not going to die. You have always been a strong and healthy woman, and I do not believe God wants you to die and leave your boys to me or anyone else."

I talked to her along these lines and then read the 103rd Psalm and said a prayer in which I prepared her to get well rather than to enter eternity. I told her to put her faith in God and throw her mind and will against every thought of dying. Then I left her, saying that I would come again after the church service. This was on a Sunday morning. I called that afternoon. Her husband met me with a smile. He said that the moment I had gone, his wife called him and the boys into the room and said, "Dr. Rose says that I am going to get well, and I am."

She did get well. But what did it? Two things: suggestion on my part and confidence on her part. I came in the nick of time, and so great was her faith in me, that I was able to inspire faith in herself. It was that faith that tipped the scales and brought her through the pneumonia. No medicine can cure pneumonia. The physicians admit it. There are cases of pneumonia that nothing can cure. We all sadly agree to that. But there are times, as in this case, when the mind, if worked upon and worked in just the right way, will turn the tide. While there is life, there is hope; but hope must be supreme and do the good that hope was created to do.

Another remarkable case: A physician asked me to see Mrs. H. He said there was nothing organically wrong with her, but she just wouldn't eat. Having made up her mind that she could not retain anything on her stomach, she had quit eating and was slowly starving herself to death. I went to see her and found, first, that she had no religious belief. She had lost her faith in God. I also found that she had no confidence in her power to retain food. My first effort was to restore her faith in the Almighty and to get her to believe that He was with her and would give her power. Then I told her that she could eat anything. True, her confidence in me was great, and my statement impressed her. She began to eat from that day! She was out of her bed in three days, for the first time in weeks. She is a normal woman today. What did it? The same forces as in the preceding case—outside suggestion and inward confidence.

There are times when the mind is sick, and it makes the body sick. At such times, it needs a stronger mind to heal it by giving it direction and especially by giving it confidence in itself. This is called suggestion. It is transmitting your confidence and power to another, and with such force as to make the other believe as you wish and do as you will. It need not be hypnotism. You can get wonderful results with patients wide awake and perfectly rational. They must believe in you, and you must know the workings of the human mind in order to meet their arguments and questionings completely and banish them utterly from their thoughts. Each one of us can be healers of this sort and, thus, help our fellows.

It is now the duty of men and women to read some of the best books on the force of the mind and learn what amazing and glorious things the mind can do to keep people well or to restore their health. We see the terrible things that wrong thinking does to people, even going to such lengths as to make them positively insane. Isn't it now high time we found out the good things that right thinking can do, and its power to cure not only mental disorders, but physical diseases as well?

I do not say that the mind can do everything. There is no reliable evidence that certain forms of real cancer have been cured by thinking or faith or any mental or religious process. I would feel myself a criminal if I led any reader to neglect the first symptoms of this awful malady by thinking to overcome them by mental suggestion. But the mind can do so much with so many, many types of human indisposition and disease that we ought to rely upon it more than we do.

Napoleon, during his campaign in Egypt, went among his soldiers who were dying by the hundreds of the black plague. He touched one of them and lifted a second, to inspire the others not to be afraid, for the awful disease seemed to be spread as much by the imagination as in any other way. Goethe tells us that he himself went where there was malignant fever and never contracted it because he put forth his will. These giants among men knew something we are slowly beginning to find out—the power of auto-suggestion. This means we have influence over ourselves by believing we cannot catch a disease or be sick. There is something about the operation of the automatic mind that rises above disease germs and bids defiance to them when we resolve not to let the thought of them frighten us or when we go in and out among the sick, even the contagiously sick, without thinking anything about it.

Imagination certainly will kill a man. There are authentic cases on record of men having actually died because they imagined they were cut with a knife across the jugular vein, when in reality, a piece of ice was used and water was allowed to drop so that they could hear it and imagine their blood was running out. They had been blindfolded before the experiment was begun. No matter how well you may be when you start for work in the morning, if everybody you meet should say to you, "How ill you look," it will not be long before you begin to feel ill, and if that thing keeps up all day, you will arrive home at night as limp as a rag and ready for a doctor. Such is the fatal power of imagination or auto-suggestion.

The first thing, then, is to remember that what pranks your imagination can play upon you, and be on your guard. Do not allow yourself to think that awful things are the matter with you or are going to be the matter with you. If you do, you will suffer.

Young medical students not infrequently think they have every disease they hear discussed or analyzed in the classroom. Some of them have imaginations so vivid that they actually come down with the disease. Yes, an imagined disease is perfectly possible and may be just as painful as a disease gotten in some other way. An imaginary pain is just as painful as any other kind of pain. No medicine can cure it. It must be removed by imagining it away.

Dr. Schofield describes the case of a woman who had a tumor. They put her on the operating table and gave her anesthetics. Lo and behold, the tumor immediately disappeared. No operation was necessary. But when she came back to consciousness, the tumor returned! The physician then learned that she had been living with a relative who had a real tumor, and her imagination was so great that she had imagined this one upon herself. She was put on the operating table again, given anesthetics, and then she was strapped around the middle so that the tumor could not artificially return. When she revived, she was told that a successful operation had been performed, but that it would be necessary to wear the bandage for several days. She believed the doctor, and when the bandage was finally removed, the tumor did not return. No operation whatever had been performed. He had simply relieved her subconscious mind, and the imagination had nothing to work upon save the idea of health, and as she had never been really sick, of course she became normal.

If what you think and brood upon can go so far as to produce an imitation tumor, do you not see how careful you should be never to imagine you have a disease of any kind?

The very best way to cure your imagination is at night, just as you go to bed. In the night season, the automatic (subconscious) mind has everything its own way, and the thoughts you give it before your day's mind (conscious mind) goes to sleep will go on working it all through the night. This may seem a foolish statement, but prove it a true one by the following test. You want to get up at seven o'clock in the morning or, say, some other hour than your regular one for rising. Now say to yourself on going to bed, "I must rise at seven o'clock." Turn that thought over to your automatic mind with absolute confidence, and you will waken at seven o'clock. This thing is done over and over again, and it is done because the subconscious self is awake all night, and when seven o'clock comes, it taps you on the shoulder, so to speak, and wakes you up. *But you must trust it.* If you have the least doubt that you will not wake up, it is likely to interfere with the whole process. Faith in your automatic mechanism causes it to operate just as you direct it before you fall asleep.

Here is a great secret, and it will help you overcome many a fault and deplorable habit. Tell yourself that you are through worrying, through drinking, through stammering, or whatever else you wish to quit, and then leave the job to the subconscious mind at night. Do this night after night, and mark my words, you will win.

SUMMARY

We have learned from this lesson that suggestion is the principle through which we may influence the minds and actions of others.

We have learned that the mind will attract to it the object it dwells upon most extensively. We have learned that the mind must be "neutralized" before it can be influenced by suggestion, and we have learned that before the mind can be "neutralized," a state of belief greater than normal must exist.

We have learned that hypnotism is nothing more than suggestion operating through a mind that has been "neutralized."

We have learned that suggestion will actually destroy body cells and develop disease, and that it will also restore body cells and destroy disease germs.

We have learned that through the principle of suggestion, we can cause a large percentage of an audience to smell peppermint when, in reality, no such odor is within smelling distance.

We have learned that confidence must be created in a person's mind before one can "neutralize" that mind. We have learned that human sympathy is a strong factor through which to build confidence, and that we can readily "neutralize" the mind of the person for whom we express full sympathy or love.

We have learned that more desirable results can be obtained (through suggestion) by complimenting a workman and caus-ing him to think well of himself than is possible through rep-rimand.

We have learned the tremendous advantage of placing our ideas and thoughts in the minds of others in such a way as to make them feel that they are the originators.

NINE

The Phenomenal Law
of Retaliation

Achieving fame or accumulating a big fortune requires the cooperation of your fellows. Whatever position one holds and whatever fortune one acquires must, to be permanent, be with the cooperation of others.

You could no more remain in a position of honor without the good will of the neighborhood than you could fly to the moon, and acquiring a big fortune without the consent of your fellows would be impossible, except by inheritance.

The peaceful enjoyment of money or position surely depends upon the extent to which you attract people to you. It does not require the farsighted philosopher to see that those who enjoy the good will of all they come in contact with can have anything that can be given by those associates.

The roadway, then, to fame and fortune—or either—leads straight through the hearts of one's fellows.

There may be other ways of gaining the good will of one's fellows that don't involve the operation of the law of retaliation, but if there is, this writer has never discovered it.

Through the law of retaliation, you can induce people to send back to you that which you give to them. There is no guesswork about this—no element of chance—no uncertainty.

Let us see just how to go about harnessing this law so it will work for us instead of against us. To begin with, we need not tell you that the tendency of the human heart is to strike back, returning, stroke for stroke, every incidence of cooperation or of antagonism.

Antagonize a person and, as surely as two and two are four, that person will retaliate in kind. Befriend a person or confer some act of kindness, and he or she will also reciprocate in kind. Never mind those who do not respond in accordance with this principle. They are merely the proverbial exception. By the law of averages, the great majority of people will quite unconsciously respond.

Those who go around with a chip on their shoulder find a dozen people a day who take delight in knocking it off, a fact to which you can easily subscribe if you have ever tried going about with a chip on your shoulder. You need no proof that the person who wears a smile and always has a word of kindness for everyone is universally liked, while the opposite type is just as generally disliked.

This law of retaliation is a powerful force that touches the whole universe, constantly attracting and repelling. You will find it in the heart of the acorn that falls to the ground and in response to the warmth of the sunlight bursts forth into a tiny sprig consisting of two small leaves that finally grow. The

acorn has attracted to itself the elements necessary to constitute a sturdy oak tree.

No one ever heard of an acorn attracting to it anything
except the cells out of which an oak tree grows. No one ever
saw a tree that was half oak and half poplar. The center of the
acorn forms affinities only with oak tree elements.

Similarly, every thought that finds abode in the human
brain attracts elements after its kind, whether of destruction
or construction, kindness or unkindness. You can no more
concentrate your mind on hatred and dislike and expect a
crop of the opposite brand than you could expect an acorn to
develop into a poplar tree. It simply is not in harmony with the
law of retaliation.

Throughout the universe, everything in the form of matter gravitates to certain centers of attraction. People of similar intellect and tendencies are attracted to each other. The
human mind forms affinities only with other minds that are
harmonious and have similar tendencies; therefore, the class
of person that you attract to you will depend upon the tendencies of your own mind. You control those tendencies and can
direct them along any line you choose, attracting to you any
sort of person you wish.

This is a law of nature. It is an immutable law, and it works
whether we make conscious use of it or not.

Another way of looking at this law is this:

The human mind resembles mother earth, in that it will
reproduce, in kind, whatever is planted in it through the five
physical senses. The tendency of the mind is to "retaliate in
kind," reciprocating all acts of kindness and resenting all acts
of injustice and unkindness. Whether acting through the

principle of suggestion or auto-suggestion, the mind directs muscular action that harmonizes with the sensory impressions it receives. Therefore, if you would have me "retaliate in kind," you can do so by placing in my mind the sensory impressions or suggestions with which I will create the necessary appropriate muscular action. Injure or displease me, and like a flash, my mind will direct appropriate muscular action, "retaliating in kind."

In studying the law of retaliation, we are carried, to an extent, into what we might call the field of unknown mental phenomena—the field of physics. The phenomena discovered in this great field have not been reduced to a science, but this shall not hinder us from making practical use of certain principles that we have discovered in this field, even though we cannot trace these principles back to first cause. One of these principles is the one we have given above as our fourth general principle of psychology, namely, "like attracts like."

No scientist has ever satisfactorily explained this principle, but the fact still remains that it is a known principle; therefore, just as we make intelligent use of electricity without knowing what it is, let us also make intelligent use of the principles of retaliation.

It is an encouraging sign to see that modern writers are giving their attention more and more to the study of the law of retaliation. Some of them call it one thing, and some call it another, but all of them seem to agree on the chief fundamental of the principle as follows:

"Like attracts like!"

The latest writer to turn her attention to this subject is Mrs. Woodrow Wilson. Her article follows:

"There seems to be a mental law to the effect that whatever generally occupies the mind is almost certain to take form in the objective. Each of us proves that in his own experience dozens of times. For instance, you may come across a word you are not familiar with. To the best of your knowledge, you have never heard it nor seen it before, and yet after your discovery of it, you will encounter it again and again.

"This fact has recently come to me in an odd sort of a way. I have been doing a great deal of reading and research on a subject which has interested me and, yet, which would certainly never be classed as live news matter. I do not remember ever having seen it mentioned in any current publication, but since I have been familiarizing myself with it, I have clipped a large number of articles treating of one phase or another of it from various magazines and newspapers.

"You can easily follow the workings of this law, whatever it is, down to the smallest details.

"A friend came to see me a day or two ago and stood transfixed upon the threshold of my sitting room.

"Flowers!" she exclaimed. "Roses?"

"There was such horror in her tones that I thought she was reproving me for buying anything but thrift stamps. She explained, however, that she was suffering from rose cold, which afflicts those who are subject to it at the same time each year, just as hay fever does.

"'It comes in June,' she said, 'when the roses are blooming, and even a whiff of their fragrance will set me sneezing for twenty minutes.'

"'It's rather a rare disease, isn't it?' I asked, after I had whisked my flowers out of sight.

"'Not at all,' she replied. 'Very common. Every other person I meet has it.'

"Now, I meet just as many people as she does during the day, perhaps more, and yet with the exception of herself, I know no one who suffers from this malady.

"Again, why is it that, if we find our thoughts turning persistently to some particular person, we are very apt to hear from him or meet him within a short time? We may not have given him a thought for months or years, and yet 'behold his shadow on the floor.'

"I know there are various explanations for these phenomena, but none of them is entirely satisfactory. The effect, however, is as if we, unconsciously to ourselves, sent out wireless messages into the universe and received the responses. Like seeks like.

"May not this account for the fact that people with grievances are always well supplied with material for fresh ones, that the mournful people have plenty to mourn about, that the most dreadful of pests, those with a chip on their shoulders, invariably arouses a burning desire in the breast of the meek and innocent bystander to knock it off?

"We all know people who are just naturally lucky.

"Everything seems to come their way. They don't have to climb trees and laboriously pick the fruit off the branches. They merely stretch out a hand, and the plums fall into it.

"I heard a woman complaining of the inequalities of fate recently and comparing her lot with that of an acquaintance.

"'Just look at her,' she said. 'Here I have worked and worried and schemed and contrived for years. Anything that I get comes by the hardest kind of effort and usually after a thousand disappointments. But she, while not half as clever as I, nor so diligent a worker, is yet a sort of a magnet attracting to her the good things that fly past me. There's no such thing as justice.'

"But she affirmed the justice of the law even while she denied it. I know the lucky woman as well as I knew the unlucky one. The difference between the two was that one was always expecting the worst and preparing for it, and the other looked forward to agreeable and pleasant things. She took them as a matter of course and made them welcome. It was always the top o' the morning to her.

"There are days, which are well known to all of us when everything goes wrong. There is certainly no malign power that is trying to thwart us and make us miserable, although it is often easier to believe so than to understand why one disturbing circumstance should follow another from early morn to evening."

One does not have to be a master of psychology to accept the truth of Mrs. Woodrow Wilson's article—it is a truth we have all experienced, yet it is a truth to which most of us have attached little or no significance.

It is in no spirit of irreverence that I place prayer, that mighty worker of miracles, in the great field of unknown phenomena. I am a firm believer in prayer! It has worked wonders for me, yet I know nothing whatsoever about the first cause to which we pray. I know this, however: that through consistent, persistent effort, prayer will break down all obstacles and force the seemingly unfathomable problems to give up their secrets!

For four years, I prayed persistently for the truth that was wrapped up in what appeared to be an impenetrable secret in another's heart. The information I wanted was known to only one other person. The very nature of the information almost necessitated its being held inviolable forever. At about the end of the fourth year, I carried my prayers a step further than I had ever done before—I determined that I would shut my eyes and behold a picture of the exact information that I wanted. Strange as it may seem, I had hardly closed my eyes before the outlines of the picture began to trace themselves in my consciousness, and within two or three minutes, I had my answer!

It seemed so strange to me that at first I believed that what I had seen was nothing but a hallucination, but I did not have to wait long before I knew better. The next day, I met the person in whose heart the secret was locked, and I was told by that person that for four years some strange force had been tugging at her heart strings, trying to induce her to tell me a story that she said she now wished to relate. In that story was the information that I wanted and for which I had prayed for four years!

Some would tell us that Divine Power produced this remarkable result, while others would be inclined to explain it through mental telepathy. My own opinion is that every thought vibration on the subject that was produced in my mind at the time of prayer was registered in the subconscious mind of the other person, having traveled through the ethereal air currents, just as vibrations travel from one instrument to another, and that these thought vibrations finally caused the alchemic change to take place in her mind, resulting in her decision to give me the information I wanted. Mind you, I said that I believe this is what took place—as to the original cause which made possible the transmission of thought through the open air, I venture no suggestions!

On another occasion, which is an extreme in the other direction, I accomplished a remarkable result through prayer in less than a minute and a half. An important business transaction was under way, and I had made an offer that had been turned down coldly. The person to whom the offer was made stepped out of his office for not longer than a minute and a half. While he was gone, I sent out a message through what we call prayer, in which I asked for a reversal of his ultimatum. He came back in and announced, without my saying a word, that he had changed his mind and would accept my offer.

Before getting away from the subject of "unknown phenomena," permit me to once more remind you that this course of scientific instruction has no connection whatsoever with any religious faith, and whenever we refer, directly or indirectly, to any subject connected with religion, we do so for purpose of comparison only.

Millions of people have found happiness and contentment through the great unknown phenomenon we call prayer. I have no desire to cause anyone to change his or her belief in prayer. To the contrary, I would do all possible to strengthen that belief!

Neither have I any intention whatsoever of reducing prayer to a purely scientific phenomenon. Whether our prayers produce such wonderful results, as we know they do, through the principle of auto-suggestion or through the influence of outside Divine forces over which we have no control is of but little importance. We are apt to pray with more *faith* and *persistence* by directing our prayers to the Divine source, and this, itself, would be one reason why we refrain from adopting the scientific principle of auto-suggestion as an explanation of the great phenomenon of prayer.

Late one afternoon, I was sitting at my desk waiting for Mrs. Hill to join me. The office staff had gone, and I was the only person in the room. I leaned over and rested my face on my hands, covering my eyes with the ends of my fingers. Mind you, I was not asleep, for I had not been in that position more than thirty seconds. Then a strange thing happened. It was almost time for Mrs. Hill to arrive. I heard her scream! I saw her knocked down by an automobile. I saw a policeman lift her up from the pavement and place her on the sidewalk. I saw the blood on her face.

I opened my eyes and looked around. I could not have been dreaming, because I was not asleep. Soon I heard Mrs. Hill's footsteps. She was excited and almost out of breath. Sure enough, she had been almost run down by an automobile at the very spot where I saw her. She did scream, and the policeman did pull her back on the sidewalk, just as I had seen him do. And, as near as we could estimate, all of this happened at the very moment when I saw it, sitting at my desk with my eyes closed, a block away from the actual scene!

In the state of Illinois, near the city of Chicago, a few years ago a farmer left his home one morning and started toward his fields to work. He had gone but a short distance when he experienced a strange feeling that impelled him to arbitrarily return to the house. He paid no attention to it at first, but it became stronger and more insistent. Finally, he could go no further, so he turned and started toward the house. The nearer he got, the faster he wanted to walk until he finally started to run. When he got inside the house, he found his daughter lying on the floor with her throat cut. Her assailant had gone but a few seconds before his arrival.

What caused these strange phenomena, we do not know, unless it was mental telepathy. These two cases are cited because both of them are authentic. I could cite more than a dozen similar cases that would tend to prove the existence of mental telepathy, by which thoughts actually pass from one mind to another, just as the vibration passes from one instrument to another through telegraphy. Of course these minds must be harmoniously attuned to each other, just as the wireless instruments must be properly attuned, or the thoughts will not register.

These examples of what we might term unknown phenomena are mentioned in connection with this lesson because we want you to stop and consider what the possibilities are for making practical use of the law of retaliation, which operates directly through the five physical senses. We do not have to depend upon unknown phenomena or mental telepathy, which are but slightly understood at this time; we can reach and influence the human mind directly through the law of retaliation and the principle of suggestion. Suggestion is the medium through which we reach the mind of another, and the law of retaliation is the principle through which we plant in that mind the seed we wish to see take root and grow.

You know what *retaliate* means! In the sense that we are using it here, it means to "return like for like," and not merely to avenge or to seek revenge, as is commonly meant by the use of this word. If I do you an injury, you retaliate at first opportunity. If I say unjust things about you, you will retaliate in kind, even in greater measure! On the other hand, if I do you a favor, you will reciprocate even in greater measure if possible.

Thus, we are following the impulse of our nature, through the "law of retaliation"!

Through the proper use of this law, I can get you to do whatever I wish you to do. If I wish you to dislike me and to lend your influence toward damaging me, I can accomplish this result by inflicting upon you the sort of treatment that I want you to inflict upon me through retaliation. If I wish your respect, your friendship, and your cooperation, I can get these by extending to you my friendship and cooperation.

On these statements, I know that we are together. You can compare these statements with your own experience, and you will see how beautifully they harmonize.

How often have you heard the remark, "What a wonderful personality that person has." How often have you met people whose personalities you coveted?

The man or woman who attracts you through a pleasing personality is merely making use of the law of harmonious attraction or the law of retaliation, both of which, when analyzed, mean that "like attracts like."

If you will study, understand, and make intelligent use of the law of retaliation, you will be an efficient and successful salesperson. When you have mastered this simple law and learned how to use it, you will have learned all that can be learned about salesmanship.

The first, and probably the most important, step to be taken in mastering this law is to cultivate complete self-control. You must learn to take all sorts of punishment and abuse without retaliating in kind. This self-control is a part of the price you must pay for mastery of the law of retaliation. When an angry person starts in to vilify and abuse you, justly or unjustly, just remember that if you retaliate in a like manner, you are being drawn down to that person's mental level; therefore, that person is dominating you!

On the other hand, if you refuse to become angry, if you retain your self-composure and remain calm and serene, you retain all your ordinary faculties of reason. You take the other by surprise. You retaliate with a weapon the other is unfamiliar with; consequently, you easily dominate.

Like attracts like! There's no denying this! Literally speaking, every person you come in contact with is a mental looking glass in which you may see a perfect reflection of your own mental attitude. As an example of direct application of the law of retaliation, let's cite an experience I recently had with my two small boys, Napoleon Junior and James.

We were on our way to the park to feed the birds and squirrels. Napoleon Junior had bought a bag of peanuts, and James had bought a box of Crackerjack. James took a notion to sample the peanuts. Without asking permission, he reached over and made a grab for the bag. He missed, and Napoleon Junior "retaliated" with his left fist, which landed rather briskly on James's jaw.

I said to James, "Now, see here, son, you didn't go about getting those peanuts in the right manner. Let me show you how to get them." It all happened so quickly that I hadn't the slightest idea what I was going to suggest to James, but I took some time to analyze the occurrence and work out a better way, if possible, than the one he adopted.

Then I thought of the experiments we had been making in connection with the law of retaliation, so I said to James, "Open your box of Crackerjack and offer your little brother some and see what happens." After considerable coaxing, I persuaded him to do this. Then a remarkable thing happened—a happening out of which I learned my greatest lesson in salesmanship! Before Napoleon Junior would touch the Crackerjack, he insisted on pouring some of his peanuts into James's overcoat pocket. He "retaliated in kind"! Out of this simple experiment with two small boys, I learned more about the art of managing them than I could have learned in any other manner. Incidentally, my boys are beginning to learn how to manipulate this law of retaliation, which saves them many a physical combat.

None of us have advanced far beyond Napoleon Junior and James as far as the operation and influence of the law of retaliation is concerned. We are all just grown-up children and easily influenced through this principle. The habit of "retaliating in kind" is so universally practiced among us that we can properly call this habit the law of retaliation. If a person presents us with a gift, we never feel satisfied. Through the principle of retaliation, we can actually convert our enemies into loyal friends. If you have an enemy whom you wish to convert into a friend, you can prove the truth of this statement if you will forget that dangerous millstone hanging around your neck that we call "pride" (stubbornness). Make a habit of speaking to this enemy with unusual cordiality. Go out of your way to favor your pride in every manner possible. Pride may seem immovable at first, but gradually will give way to your influence and "retaliate in kind"! The hottest coals of fire ever heaped upon the head of one who has wronged you are the coals of human kindness.

How true it is that "we receive only that which we give"! It is not what we wish that comes back to us, but what we give.

I implore you to make use of this law, not alone for material gain, but, better still, for the attainment of happiness and good will toward men.

This, after all, is the only real success to strive for.

SUMMARY

In this lesson we have learned a great principle—probably the most important major principle of psychology! We have learned that our thoughts and actions toward others resemble an electric magnet which attracts to us the same sort of thought and the same sort of action that we, ourselves, create.

We have learned that "like attracts like," whether in thought or in expression of thought through bodily action. We have learned that the human mind responds in kind to whatever thought impressions it receives. We have learned that the human mind resembles mother earth in that it will reproduce a crop of muscular action which corresponds, in kind, to the sensory impressions planted in it. We have learned that kindness begets kindness, and unkindness and injustice beget unkindness and injustice.

We have learned that our actions toward others, whether of kindness or unkindness, justice or injustice, come back to us in even larger measure! We have learned that the human mind responds in kind to all sensory impressions it receives; therefore, we know what we must do to influence any desired action upon the part of another. We have learned that "pride" and "stubbornness" must be brushed away before we can make use of the law of retaliation in a constructive way.

Why is it that when once a man begins to make money, the whole world seems to beat a pathway to his door? Take any person you know who enjoys financial success, and he will tell you that he is being constantly sought, and that opportunities to make money are constantly being urged upon him!

"To him that hath shall be given, but to him that hath not shall be taken away even that which he hath" (Matthew 25:29). This quotation from the Bible used to seem ridiculous to me, yet how true it is when reduced to its concrete meaning. Yes, *"to him that hath shall be given"*! If he "hath" failure, lack of self-confidence, hatred, or lack of self-control, to him shall these qualities be given in still greater abundance! But, if he "hath" success, self-confidence, self-control, patience, and persistence, to him shall these qualities be increased!

Sometimes it may be necessary to meet force with force until we overpower our opponent or adversary, but while he is down is a splendid time to complete the "retaliation" by taking him by the hand and showing him a better way to settle disputes. Like attracts like! Germany once sought to bathe her sword in human blood, in a ruthless escapade of conquest. As a result, she drew the "retaliation in kind" of most of the civilized world.

It is for you to decide what you want others to do, and it is for you to get them to do it through the law of retaliation.

TEN

The Power of Your Chameleon Mind

This lesson brings us to the next general principle of psychology, which we will state as follows.

Environment: The human mind has a decided tendency to absorb the environment with which we are surrounded, and to cause bodily activity that harmonizes with and is appropriate to that environment. The mind feeds on and grows to resemble the sense impressions it absorbs from the environment in which we live. The mind resembles a chameleon, in that it changes its color to correspond to its environment. None but the strongest minds will resist the tendency to absorb the surrounding environment.

Habit: Habit grows out of environment—out of doing the same thing in the same way repeatedly—out of thinking the same thoughts over and over—and when once formed, it resembles cement that has set in its molds and is hard to break.

Thought and action are built from the material drawn from the surrounding environment by the mind. Habit crystallizes these into permanent fixtures of our personality and stores them away in our subconscious minds. Habit may be likened to the grooves on an old phonograph record, while the human mind may be likened to the needle point that fits into that groove. When any habit has been well formed (by repetition of thought or action), the mind has a tendency to attach itself to and follow that habit as closely as the phonograph needle follows the groove in the record.

We begin to see, therefore, the importance of selecting our environment with the greatest possible care, because it is the mental feeding grounds out of which the stuff that goes into our minds is to be extracted. Environment supplies the food and the materials out of which we create thought, and habit crystallizes these materials into permanency!

For this very reason, under our present system of handling criminals, we create more of them than we cure! When the subjects of environment and habit are better understood, our entire penal system will receive a well-deserved overhauling and transformation. We will stop penning men together like so many cattle, all branded with the stripe of disgrace that ever reminds them that they are "criminals"! We will place offenders in a clean atmosphere, where every part of the environment will suggest to them that they are being transformed into useful human beings, instead of placing them where they are constantly reminded that they are offenders of society. In this age of advancement and human intelligence, the prison ought to be considered a hospital in which perverted and deranged mentalities are nursed back to normal. The old idea of punishment for crime ought to be replaced by the new and more advanced idea of cure for crime. The law of retaliation, suggestion, auto-suggestion, and the other principles covered by this course will each play its part in doing away with punishment and adopting cure as a means of transforming criminals back to normal.

The honor system, as adopted in a limited way in many of our penal institutions, is a step in the right direction. The parole system is another step forward. The time is rapidly approaching when every offender of the laws of society will be sent, not to dark, repellant, dirty, and filthy prison cells, but directly to the laboratory of the mental hospital where the mind as well as the body of the unfortunate one will receive attention and proper treatment.

This reform in prison methods is going to be one of the great reforms of the present age! And psychology is going to be the medium through which this reform will operate. In fact, after psychology becomes one of the regularly taught subjects in our public schools, the criminal tendencies that the growing child absorbs from its environment will be effectively counterbalanced through the principles of psychology.

But we must not digress too far from the subjects of our lesson: habit and environment. Let us learn more about the characteristics of habit from the following words of Edward E. Beals, one of the world's leading psychologists.

HABIT

"Habit is a force which is generally recognized by the average thinking person, but which is commonly viewed only in its adverse aspect. It has been well said that all are 'the creatures of habit,' and that 'habit is a cable; we weave a thread of it each day, and it becomes so strong that we cannot break it.' But the above quotations only serve to emphasize that side of the question in which people are shown as the slaves of habit, suffering from its confining bonds. There is another side to the question, and that side shall be considered in this chapter.

"If it be true that habit becomes a cruel tyrant, ruling and compelling people against their will, desire, and inclination—and this is true in many cases—the question naturally arises in the thinking mind whether this mighty force cannot be harnessed and controlled in the service of humanity, just as have other forces of nature. If this result can be accomplished, then people may master habit and set it to work, instead of being a slave to it and serving it faithfully, though complaining. And the modern psychologists tell us in no uncertain tones that habit may certainly be thus mastered, harnessed, and set to work, instead of being allowed to dominate one's actions and character. And thousands of people have applied this new knowledge and have turned the force of habit into new channels, and have compelled it to work their machinery of action, instead of being allowed to run to waste, or else permitted to sweep away the structures that mankind has erected with care and expense, or to destroy fertile mental fields.

"A habit is a 'mental patch' over which our actions have traveled for some time, each passing making the path a little deeper and a little wider. If you have to work over a field or through a forest, you know how natural it is for you to choose the clearest path in preference to the less worn ones, and greatly in preference to stepping out across the field or through the woods and making a new path. And the line of mental action is precisely the same. It is movement along the lines of the least resistance—passage over the well-worn path.

"Habits are created by repetition and are formed in accordance to a natural law, observable in all animate things, and some would say in inanimate things as well. As an instance of the latter, it is pointed out that a piece of paper, once folded in a certain manner, will fold along the same lines every time.

"The following rules will help you in your work in forming new habits:

1. At the beginning of the formation of a new habit, put force into your expression of the action, thought, or characteristic. Remember that you are taking the first steps toward making the new mental path, and it is much harder at the first than it will be afterwards. Make the path as clear and deep as you can at the start, so that you can see it readily the next time you wish to travel it.

2. Keep your attention firmly concentrated on the new path you are building, and keep your eyes and thoughts away from the old paths, lest you incline toward them. Forget all about the old paths, and concern yourself only with the new one that you are building.

3. Travel over your newly made path as often as possible. Make opportunities for doing so, without waiting for them to arise. The more often you go over the new path, the sooner will it become an old, well-worn, easily traveled one.

4. Resist the temptation to travel over the older, easier paths that you have been using in the past. Every time you resist a temptation, the stronger do you become, and the easier will it be for you to do so the next time. But every time you yield to the temptation, the easier does it become to yield again, and the more difficult does it become to resist the next time. You will have a fight at the start, and this is the critical time. Prove your determination, persistency, and willpower now, right here at the start. As all users of sewing machines or other delicate pieces of mechanism know, as a machine or instrument is once 'broken in,' so will it tend to run thereafter? The same law is also observable in the case of musical instruments. Clothing or gloves form into creases according to the person using them, and these creases, once formed, will always be in effect, notwithstanding repeated pressings. Rivers and streams of water cut their courses through the land and, thereafter, flow along the habit-course. The law is in operation everywhere.

5. Be sure that you have mapped out the proper path—plan it out well, and see where it will lead you to—then go ahead without fear and without allowing yourself to doubt. 'Place your hand upon the plow, and look not backward.' Select your goal—then make a good, deep, wide mental path leading straight to it."

The above illustrations will help you to form the idea of the nature of habit and will aid you in forming new mental paths—new mental creases. And, remember this always—the best (and one might say the only) way in which old habits may be removed is to form new habits to counteract and replace the undesirable ones. Form new mental paths over which to travel, and the old ones will soon become less distinct and, in time, will practically fill up from disuse. Every time you travel over the path of the desirable mental habit, you make the path deeper and wider, and make it so much easier to travel it thereafter. This mental path-making is a very important thing, and I cannot urge upon you too strongly the injunction to start to work making the desirable mental paths over which you wish to travel. Practice, practice, practice—be a good path-maker.

There is a close resemblance between habit and auto-suggestion. Through habit, an act repeatedly performed in the same manner has a tendency to become permanent, and eventually we perform the act automatically and without much thought or concentration. In playing a piano, for example, the player can play a familiar piece while his or her conscious mind is on some other subject.

Through auto-suggestion, as we have already learned from previous lessons, a thought, idea, ambition, or desire held constantly in the mind eventually claims the greater portion of the conscious mind and, accordingly, causes appropriate muscular action of the body to the end that the idea so held may be transformed into physical reality. Auto-suggestion, therefore, is the first principle we use in forming habits. We form habits through the principle of auto-suggestion, and we can destroy habits through the same principle.

All you need to do in forming or eliminating any habit is to make use of the principle of auto-suggestion with persistence. A mere fleeting wish is not auto-suggestion at all. An idea or desire, to be transformed into reality, must be held in the conscious mind faithfully and persistently until it begins to take permanent form.

What is needed is a steady, determined, persistent application to the one object upon which you have set your mind. Having found the object of your desire and knowing how to concentrate upon it, you should then learn how to be persistent in your concentration, aim, and purpose. There is nothing like sticking to a thing. Many are brilliant, resourceful, and industrious, but they fail to reach the goal by reason of their lack of "stick-to-it-tiveness." One should acquire the tenacity of the bulldog, and refuse to be shaken off a thing once attention and desire are fixed upon it. You remember the old Western hunter who, when once he had gazed upon an animal and said, "You're my meat," would never leave the trail or pursuit of that animal if he had to track it for weeks, losing his meat in the meantime. Such a man would, in time, acquire such a faculty of persistence that the animals feel like Davy Crockett's sidekick, who cried out, "Don't shoot, mister, I'll come down without it."

You know the dogged persistence inherent in some that strikes us as an irresistible force when we meet them and causes conflict with their persistent determination. We are apt to call this the "will," but it is our old friend persistence—that faculty of holding the will firmly up against objects, just as the workman holds the chisel against the object on the wheel, never taking off the pressure of the tool until the desired result is obtained.

No matter how strong a will people may have, if they have not learned the art of the persistent application of it, they fail to obtain the best results. One must learn to acquire that constant, unvarying, unrelenting application to the object of desire that will enable him or her to hold the will firmly against the object until it is shaped accordingly. Not only today and tomorrow, but every day until the end.

Sir Thomas Fowell Buxton has said, "The longer I live, the more certain I am that the great difference between the feeble and the powerful, the great and the insignificant, is energy—invincible determination—a purpose once fixed, and then death or victory. That quality will do anything that can be done in this world—and no talents, no circumstances, no opportunities, will make a two-legged creature a human without it."

Donald G. Mitchell said, "Resolve is what makes one manifest, not puny resolve, not crude determinations, not errant purposes—but that strong and indefatigable will which treads down difficulties and danger, as a boy treads down the heaving frost-lands of winter, which kindles his eye and brain with proud pulse-beat toward the unattainable. Will makes giants."

Disraeli said, "I have brought myself, by long meditation, to the conviction that a human being with a settled purpose must accomplish it, and that nothing can resist a will which will stake even existence upon its fulfillment."

Sir John Simpson said, "A passionate desire and an unwearied will can perform impossibilities, or what may seem to be such to the cold and feeble."

And John Foster adds his testimony when he says, "It is wonderful how even the casualties of life seem to bow to a spirit that will not bow to them, and yield to observe a design which they may, in their first apparent tendency, threaten to frustrate, when a firm, decisive spirit is recognized; it is curious to see how the space clears around such a spirit and leaves room and freedom."

Abraham Lincoln said of General Grant, "The great thing about him is cool persistency of purpose. He is not easily excited, and he has got the grip of a bulldog. When he once gets his teeth in, nothing can shake him off."

Now, you may object that the above quotations relate to the will, rather than to persistence. But if you stop to consider a moment, you will see that they relate to the persistent will, and that the will without persistence could accomplish none of these things claimed for it. The will is the hard chisel, but persistence is the mechanism that holds the chisel in its place, firmly pressing it up against the object to be shaped, and keeping it from slipping or relaxing its pressure. You cannot closely read the above quotations from these great authorities without feeling a tightness of your lips and setting of your jaw, the outward marks of the persistent, dogged will.

If you lack persistence, you should begin to train yourself in the direction of acquiring the habit of sticking to things. This practice will establish a new habit of the mind, and will also tend to cause the appropriate brain cells to develop and, thus, give to you as a permanent characteristic the desired quality that you are seeking to develop. Fix your mind upon your daily tasks, studies, occupation, or hobbies, and hold your attention firmly upon them by concentration, until you find yourself getting into the habit of resisting "sidetracking" or distracting influences. It is all a matter of practice and habit. Carry in your mind the idea of the chisel held firmly against the object it is shaping, as given in this lesson—it will help you so much. And read this over and over again, every day or so, until your mind will take up the idea and make it its own. By so doing, you will tend to arouse the desire for persistence, and the rest will follow naturally, as the fruit follows the budding and flowering of the tree.

Persistence may be compared to the "drop of water which finally wears away the hardest stone." When the final chapter of your lifework is written, you will find that your persistence, or lack of it, has played a mighty part in your success or failure.

In hundreds of thousands of cases, people's talents could be matched, one against the other, with the result that there would be no noticeable difference in their ability to accomplish a desired end. One has as much education as the other. One has as much latent ability as the other. They go forth into the world with equal chances of winning their goals, but one succeeds and the other fails! Accurate analysis will show that the one succeeded because of persistence, while the other failed because he or she lacked persistence!

Persistence, auto-suggestion, and habit are a trio of words whose meaning no one can afford to overlook. Persistence is the strong cord that binds auto-suggestion and habit together until they merge into one and become a permanent reality.

In the First World War, the chief strategic value of the German propaganda lay in the fact that it broke down the spirit of those it was directed against. In other words, it broke down the persistence! The Prussian sent to destroy the author of these lessons and render his educational work unimportant made extensive use of this principle of destroying his persistence by breaking his spirit. Silently and subtly, this trained agent of the Kaiser set about turning the author's friends and business associates against him. Well did he know the necessity of destroying the power of persistence! To crush the spirit and break down the persistence of those who stand in his way is a strong factor in the German propagandist's work. To destroy the "morale"—in other words, the persistence—of an army is of strategic importance of great value. Destroy the morale of an army, and you have defeated that army! The same rule applies to a smaller group of individuals, or to one person.

We can only develop persistence through absolute self-confidence! This is why we have laid so much stress upon the value of the lesson on self-confidence, and why we have commended that lesson to you as being the most important lesson of applied psychology. There is a central idea around which that lesson is built, which shows you exactly how to use whatever latent ability you have, and how to supplement this with whatever faith you have in the infinite.

Go back to that lesson and ponder over it!

Behind those simple lines, you will find the secret of achievement, the key to the Mysteries of an indomitable will power! Stripped of all technicalities, you will find in that lesson "that subtle something" that will vitalize your brain and send that radiant glow through your whole body, that thing that will cause you to want to grab your hat, go out, and do something!

The greatest service that any teacher can perform for you is to cause you to arouse that sleeping genius inside of your brain and inspire it with the ambition to accomplish some worthy undertaking! It is not what education or schooling puts in your head that will benefit you, but what is aroused in you and put to work!

Persistence on your part will eventually arouse that indescribable something, whatever it is, and when it is once aroused, you will sweep all obstacles before you and swiftly ride on to the achievement of your desired goal, on the wings of this newly found power that you had within you all the time, but didn't know it! And when you once discover this irresistible power that sleeps in your brain, no one on earth can again dominate you or use you as a piece of putty. You will then have discovered your tremendous mental power, just as a horse discovers a superior physical power when he once runs away. Ever afterward, you will refuse to be haltered and ridden by any human being on earth!

If you follow the plan laid down in the theme around which these lessons are built, you are sure to find this great power. You will have then come to yourself. You will have discovered the true principle through which the human race has gradually, throughout ages, risen above the animals of the lower stages of evolution.

ENVIRONMENT

As we have already said, we absorb sense impressions from our surrounding environment. Environment, in the sense that we use it here, covers a very broad field. It embraces the books we read, the people with whom we associate, the community in which we live, the nature of the work in which we are engaged, the country in which we reside, the clothes we wear, the songs we sing, and the thoughts we think! The purpose of our discussion of the subject of environment is to show its direct relationship to the personality we are developing in ourselves, and the importance of creating an environment out of which we can develop the "chief aim" on which we have set our hearts!

The mind feeds upon what we supply it with, through our environment; therefore, let us select our environment with the direct object of supplying the mind with suitable material, with which it will carry on its work of realizing our "chief aim."

If your environment is not to your liking, change it! The first step to be taken is to create in your own mind an exact picture of the environment in which you believe you could do your best work, and from which you would probably draw those emotional feelings and qualities that would tend to urge you on toward your desired goal.

The first step you must take in every accomplishment is the creation, in the mind, of an exact outline or picture of that which you intend to build in reality. This is something you cannot afford to forget! This great truth applies to the building of a desirable environment just the same as it does to everything else that you desire to create.

Your daily associates constitute the most important and influential part of your environment, whether toward your progress or your failure. It will be of much benefit to you to select as your associates, people who are in sympathy with your aims and ideals, and whose mental attitude inspires you with enthusiasm, determination, and ambition. If, perchance, you have on your list of associates a person who never sees anything except the negative side of life—a person who is always complaining and whining—a person who talks about failure and the shortcomings of humanity—erase such a person from your list as soon as you possibly can.

Every word uttered within your hearing, every sight that reaches your eyes, and every sense impression that you receive in any other manner influences your thought as surely as the sun rises in the east and sets in the west! This being true, can you not see how important it is to control, as far as possible, the sense impressions that reach your mind? Can you not see the importance also of controlling, as far as possible, the environment in which you live? Can you not see the importance of reading books that deal with subjects that have a direct bearing on your "chief aim"? Can you not see the importance of talking with people who are in sympathy with you and your aims—people who will encourage you and urge you on to greater effort?

Through the principle of suggestion, every word uttered within your hearing and every sight within the gaze of your eyes is influencing your action. You are either consciously or unconsciously absorbing, assimilating, or making a part of yourself the ideas, thoughts, and acts of your associates. Constant association with evil minds will, in time, mold your own mind in conformity with that of the evil one. This is the chief reason why we should avoid "bad" company. The fact that association with disreputable people will bring you into disrepute in the minds of others is, within itself, sufficient reason for your avoiding such associates, but the more important reason why you should do this is the fact that you are constantly absorbing the ideas of your associates and making them a part of your own!

The leading scientists of the world are agreed that nature has been millions of years in creating, through the process of evolution, our present civilized environment as it is represented by the present state of intellectual and physical development. We have only to stop and consider what environment will do, in less than a score of years, what it took nature, in her process of evolution, thousands of years to accomplish, to see the powerful influence of environment. A savage baby, reared by its savage parents, remains a savage; but that same baby, if reared by a refined, civilized family, throws off its savage tendencies, and all but a few of its savage instincts, absorbing its civilized environment in one generation.

On the other hand, the race descends as rapidly as it ascends, through the influence of environment. In war, for example, refined soldiers, who, under ordinary circumstances, would shudder at the thought of killing a human being, become enthusiastic slayers, actually taking delight in the act. It requires but a few months of preparation in a "war environment" to take a soldier backward in evolution.

The clothes you wear also influence you; thereby, they form a part of your environment. Soiled or shabby clothes depress you and lower your self-confidence, while clean, modest, and refined clothes give you a sort of inner feeling of courage that causes you to quicken your step as you walk. We need not tell you what a difference there is in the way you feel in your work clothes and your casual clothes, for you have noticed this difference many a time. You either want to shrink away from people who are better dressed than you, or you meet people on an equal basis, with courage and self-confidence. Therefore, not only do others judge us by our clothes at first meeting, but we judge ourselves to a large extent by our clothes. As evidence of this, witness the feeling of discomfort and depression that we experience if our under-clothing is soiled, even though our other garments are in perfect condition and of the latest design, and our under-clothes cannot be seen.

While we are on the subject of clothes, I want to relate an experience I once had which brought home to me very forcefully the tremendous part clothes play in one's mental courage or lack of it. I was once invited into the laboratory of a well-known teacher of physical fitness. While I was there, he persuaded me to take off my clothes and accept, gratis, a simple treatment. After the treatment was over, I was ushered into his presence by an attendant, in a well-appointed office, wearing nothing except the pair of trunks in which I had taken my treatment. On the opposite side of a large mahogany desk sat my friend, the teacher, attired in a neat formal business suit. The contrast between him and me was so great and so unavoidably noticeable that it embarrassed me. I felt a great deal like I imagine the near-sighted man felt who once made the mistake of stepping out of his dressing room into a crowded ballroom, thinking that he was going into a closet where his clothes were.

It was no mere accident that I was ushered into the presence of this teacher in scanty attire! He was a practical psychologist, and he well knew the effect it would have on a prospective purchaser of his course to be placed at such a disadvantage. The reception had been "staged," in other words, and the chief actor who was very efficiently directing the play was the man on the other side of the desk who had on proper clothes. With this setting, this teacher canvassed me to purchase his course, which I did. After I got back into my regular clothes and into my usual environment and analyzed the visit, I could plainly see that the sale was an easy matter under the setting that this man had very ingeniously prepared.

Good clothes affect us in two ways. First, they give us greater courage and more self-confidence, which alone would justify us in providing ourselves with proper clothes, even to the exclusion of some other necessity of less value. Second, they impress others in our favor. The first sensory impression that reaches the minds of those we meet reaches them through the sense of sight, as they quickly look us over and take mental inventory of hat they see. In this way, a person often forms an opinion of us, good, bad, or indifferent, before we utter a word, based entirely upon the impression our clothes and the manner in which we wear them make upon his or her mind.

Money invested in good clothes is not a luxury, but a sound business investment that will pay the best of dividends. We simply cannot afford to neglect our personal appearance, both for the effect it will have on us and for the effect it will have upon those with whom we come in contact socially, commercially, or professionally. Good clothes are not an extravagance—they are a necessity! These statements are based upon scientifically sound principles. The most important part of our physical environment is that which we create by the clothes we wear, because this particular part of our environment affects both ourselves and all we come in contact with.

Next to our clothes, an important factor in the surroundings that constitute our environment is the office or shop in which we work. Experiments have proved conclusively that an employee is influenced very decidedly by the harmony, or lack of it, that is present during working hours. A disorganized, chaotic, dirty shop or office tends to depress employees and lower their enthusiasm and interest in work, whereas a well-organized, clean, and systematic workplace has just the opposite effect. Employers who, in recent years, have come to understand how to employ the principles of psychology to increase the efficiency of their employees have learned the advantage, in dollars and cents, of providing clean, comfortable, harmonious shops and offices.

Whenever increased human efficiency takes place at all, it begins in the human mind! Workers produce greater results because they want to do so! Now, the problem is to find ways and means, devices and equipment, environment and surroundings, atmosphere and working conditions with which to make men and women want to do more work and better work! Environment is the first thing the really efficient "efficiency counselor" takes notice of. No one can be a competent efficiency counselor without being also a psychologist.

I am thoroughly convinced, after taking a retrospective view of my experience as a boy on a farm, that if I were engaged in the business of farming and had to depend upon boys to help me do the work, I would provide a baseball field nearby and such other games as boys like to engage in, and every so often we would finish a given task or a pre-arranged piece of work and then head to the ball ground for a little turn at the "enthusiasm builder"! With this incentive, a boy (and most of us are only boys and girls grown tall) would produce more work and experience less fatigue than he would without it. That old axiom, "all work and no play makes Jack a dull boy" is more than an axiom—it is a scientific truth with teeth in it!

Somewhere, sometime, some foreman, superintendent, or manager will read this lesson and see the practical value of entertaining people while they work and of providing them with a pleasing, harmonious environment. Not only will he or she see the practical value of the idea, but better still, will put it into use, and it will carry him or her into prominent leadership!

Perhaps you are that man or woman!

If you have faithfully put into practice the suggestions laid down in the lesson on self-confidence building, you are undoubtedly headed in the direction of leadership. What you now need is some big idea with which to complete the journey. It may be that on these pages you will find that idea!

One big idea is all that any person really needs or can make use of in this life. Too many of us go through life with plenty of little ideas clinging to us, but with no really big idea! When you find your big idea, more likely than not, you will find it in some sort of service that will be of constructive help to your fellows! It may be the idea of lowering the cost to the consumer of some necessity of life; or, it may be the idea of helping men and women to discover the wonderful power of the human mind and how to make use of it; or, it may be the idea of helping people to be more cheerful and happy in their work by creating some plan for improving their working environment. If it doesn't promise some of these results, you may be reasonably sure that it is not a big idea.

What more worthy cause could you devote your life to than that of helping to improve the environment of those who earn their living with their hands? It may be that this field of effort does not always yield as great a return in dollars and cents, but certain it is that its workers enjoy that serene, harmonious mental environment which is always experienced by those who give their lives for the uplift and the enlightenment of humanity. Incidentally, this brings us to a suitable point at which to discuss the last phase of environment, which is mental environment.

Up to this point, we have been discussing the purely physical side of environment, such as the clothes we wear, the equipment with which we work, the room in which we work, the people with whom we associate, and the like. But as between the mental and the physical sides of environment, the mental side is of greater importance. Our mental environment is represented by the condition of our minds. In the last analysis, the physical environment is merely the material out of which we create our mental environment. The exact state of mind existing at any given time is the result of sense impressions which have reached the mind from the physical environment, at one time or another, and constitutes our mental environment.

We can rise above and beyond a negative physical environment by creating in our imagination a positive one, or by shutting out all thought of it altogether, but a negative mental environment cannot be dodged—it must be rebuilt. Out of our mental environment, we create every impulse leading to bodily action; therefore, if our muscular, bodily activities are wisely directed, they must emanate from a sound mental environment. Hence, we claim that as between the mental and physical environments, the former is of greater importance.

SUMMARY

We have learned from this lesson the part environment and habit play in one's success or failure. We have learned that there are two phases of environment, one mental and the other physical, and that the mental side is created out of the physical. We have learned, therefore, the importance of controlling, as far as possible, the physical environment, because it is the raw material out of which we build the mental environment.

We have learned how to make and to unmake habit, through persistence and auto-suggestion. We have learned that both auto-suggestion and concentration play an important part in the creation of any habit.

We have learned that the tendency of the human mind is to absorb its surrounding environment. We have learned, therefore, that environment is the raw material out of which we are shaping our ideas and our characters. We have learned that so forceful is the environment in which we live that a sound mind may absorb criminal tendencies by improper association with criminal minds, through inadequate penal institutions, and so on.

We have learned that the clothes we wear constitute an important part of our physical environment, and that they influence us as well as those with whom we come in contact, either negatively or positively, according to their appropriateness.

We have learned the importance of providing workers with a pleasing, harmonious physical environment, and of the increased efficiency that results.

ELEVEN

The Lessons My Failures
Have Taught Me

have often heard the expression, "If I had my life to live over, I would live it differently." However, I could not truthfully say that I would change anything that has happened in my life if I were living it over. Not that I have made no mistakes, for indeed it seems to me that I have made more mistakes than the average person makes, but out of these mistakes has come an awakening that has brought me real happiness and abundant opportunity to help others find this much sought state of mind.

I am convinced, beyond room for doubt, that there is a great lesson in every failure, and that so-called failure is absolutely necessary before worthwhile success can be attained.

I am convinced that a part of nature's plan is to throw obstacles in our pathways, just as the trainer lays down rails and hurdles for a horse to jump over while being trained to "pace," and that the greatest part of one's education comes not from books or teachers, but from constantly striving to over-come these obstacles.

In this chapter I will do my best to set down for the readers some of the lessons that my failures have taught me.

Let us begin with my favorite hobby—namely, putting into practice my belief that the only real happiness anyone ever experiences comes from helping others to find happiness. It may be a mere coincidence that practically twenty-five of my thirty-six years were very unhappy years, and that I began to find happiness the very day I began to help others find it, but I do not believe so. I believe this is more than a coincidence—I believe that it is in strict accordance with a law of the universe.

NO SOWING GRIEF
AND REAPING HAPPINESS

My experience has taught me that a person can no more sow a crop of grief and expect to reap a harvest of happiness than they could sow thistles and expect to reap a crop of wheat. Through many years of careful study and analysis, I have learned con-clusively that what a person gives comes back increased many times, even down to the finest detail, whether a mere thought or an overt act.

Likewise, as I have said, from a material, economic stand-point, one of the greatest truths I have learned is that it pays handsomely to render more service and better service than one is paid to render, for just as surely as this is done, it is but a ques-tion of time until one is paid for more than one actually does.

This practice of throwing one's heart into every task, regardless of the remuneration, will go further toward the achievement of material, monetary success than any other one thing I could mention. But this is hardly of less importance than the habit of forgiving and forgetting the wrongs others commit against us. The habit of "striking back" at those who anger us is a weakness that is bound to degrade and work to the detriment of all who practice it.

I am convinced that no lesson that my life's experience has taught me has been more costly than the one I learned by eternally exacting my "pound of flesh" and feeling it my duty to resent every insult and every injustice.

GREAT LEADERS CURB THEIR ANGER

I am thoroughly convinced that one of the greatest lessons a person can learn is that of self-control. One can never exercise any very great amount of influence over others until he or she first learns to exercise control over the self. It seems to me of particular significance, when I stop and consider that most of the world's great leaders have been people slow to anger and that the greatest of all the leaders down the ages who gave us the greatest philosophy the world has ever known, as it is laid down in the Golden Rule, was a person of tolerance and self-control.

I am convinced that it is a grievous mistake for people to start out with the belief that upon their shoulders rests the burden of "reforming" the world, or of changing the natural order of human conduct. I believe that nature's own plans are working out quite rapidly enough without the interference of those who would presume to try to rush nature or in any way divert her course. Such presumption leads only to argument, contention, and ill feelings.

I have learned, to my own satisfaction at least, that a person who agitates and works up ill feeling, for any cause whatsoever, serves no real constructive purpose in life. It pays to boost and construct instead of knocking and tearing down.

When I began writing magazine articles, I commenced making use of this principle by devoting my time and editorial pages to that which is constructive and overlooking that which is destructive.

Nothing I have ever undertaken in all of my thirty-six years has proved as successful or brought me as much real happiness as my work on this little magazine has done.

Almost from the very day that the first edition went on the newsstands, success has crowned my efforts in greater abundance than I had ever hoped for. Not necessarily monetary success, but that higher, finer success which is manifested in the happiness that my magazine articles have helped others to find.

I have found, from many years of experience, that it is a sign of weakness to permit oneself to be influenced against another person on account of some remark made by an enemy or someone who is prejudiced. A person cannot truly claim to possess self-control or the ability to think clearly until he or she learns to form opinions of others not from someone else's viewpoint, but from actual knowledge.

ONE BAD HABIT I DON'T MISS

One of the most detrimental and destructive habits I have had to overcome has been that of allowing myself to be influenced against a person by someone who was biased or prejudiced.

I have learned, by having made the same mistake over and over again, is that it is a grievous mistake to slander others, either with or without cause. I cannot recall any personal development I have gained from my mistakes that has given me as much real satisfaction as what I have experienced from the knowledge that I had, to some extent, learned to hold my tongue unless I could say something kind of my fellows.

I only learned to curb this natural human tendency of "picking one's enemies to pieces" after I began to understand the law of retaliation, through the operation of which a person is sure to reap what they sow, either by word of mouth or by action.

I am by no means master of this evil, but I have at least made a fair start toward conquering it.

My experience has taught me that most people are inherently honest, and that those whom we usually call dishonest are victims of circumstances over which they haven't full control.

It has been a source of great benefit to me in editing the magazine stories to know that it is a natural tendency of people to live up to the reputation others give them.

I am convinced that every person should go through that biting, though valuable, experience of having been attacked by the newspapers and losing their fortune, at least once in a lifetime, because it is when calamity overtakes that they learn who are their real friends. The friends stay by the ship while the wannabees make for cover.

I have learned, among other interesting bits of knowledge of human nature, that a people can be very accurately judged by the character of those they attract to themselves. That old axiomatic phrase, "birds of a feather flock together," is sound philosophy.

THE LAW OF ATTRACTION AT WORK

Throughout the universe this law of attraction, as it might be called, continuously attracts things of a like nature. A great detective once told me that this law of attraction was his chief dependence in hunting down criminals and those charged with breaking the law.

I have learned that those who aspire to be public servants must be prepared to sacrifice much and withstand abuse and criticism without losing faith in or respect in their fellowmen. It is rare indeed to find a person engaged in serving the public whose motives are not questioned by the very people whom his efforts benefit most.

The greatest servant the world has ever known not only gained the ill will of many of the people of his time—an ill will to which a great many of the present age have fallen heir—but he lost his life in the bargain. They nailed him to a cross, pierced his side with a spear, and fiendishly tortured him by spitting in his face while his life slowly ebbed away. He set us a mighty fine example to follow in his last words, which were something like, "Forgive them, Father, for they know not what they do."

When I feel my blood rushing to my head in anger on account of the wrongs that people do me, I find comfort in the fortitude and the patience with which the great philosopher watched his tormentors as they slowly put him to death for no offense whatsoever except that of trying to help his fellowmen find happiness.

My experience has taught me that those who accuse the world of not giving them a chance to succeed in their chosen work instead of pointing the accusing finger at themselves, seldom find their name in Who's Who.

A "chance to succeed" is something every person must go out and create for themselves. Without a certain degree of combativeness, a person is not apt to accomplish very much in this world or acquire anything that other people covet very highly. Without combativeness, people can easily inherit poverty, misery, and failure, but if they get a grip on the opposite to these, they must be prepared to "contend" for their rights.

But note well that I said "rights."

The only "rights" we have are those we create in return for service rendered, and it may not be a bad idea to remind ourselves that the nature of those "rights" will correspond exactly to the nature of the service rendered.

My experience has taught me that a child can be burdened with no heavier a load, nor visited with a greater curse, than that which accompanies the indiscriminate use of wealth. A close analysis of history will show that most of the great servants of the public and of humanity were people who arose from poverty.

THE TEST OF GREAT WEALTH

In my opinion, a real test is to give someone unlimited wealth and see what he or she does with it. Wealth that takes away the incentive to engage in constructive, useful work is a curse to those who so use it. It is not poverty that a person needs to watch out for—it is wealth and the attendant power that wealth creates, for good or for evil ends.

I consider it very fortunate that I was born in poverty, while in my more mature years I have associated rather closely with people of wealth; thus I have had a very fair demonstration of the effect of these two widely separated positions. I know I shall not need to watch myself so very closely as long as the need for life's ordinary necessities confronts me, but if I should gain great wealth, it would be quite essential for me to see that this did not take away the desire to serve my fellowmen.

My experience has taught me that a normal person can accomplish anything possible, through the aid of the human mind. The greatest thing the mind can do is to imagine! The so-called genius is merely a person who has created something definite through imagination, and then transformed that picture into reality through action.

All this, and a little more, have I learned during these past thirty-six years. But the greatest thing I have learned is that old, old truth which the philosophers all down the ages have told us: that happiness is found not in possessions, but in useful service!

This is a truth that we can appreciate only after having discovered it for ourselves.

There may be many ways through which I could find greater happiness than what I receive in return for the work I devote to the editing of my magazine, but frankly, I have not discovered it, nor do I expect to.

The only thing I can think of that would bring me a greater measure of happiness than I already have would be a larger number of people to serve through this little brown-covered messenger of good cheer and enthusiasm.

NEVER HEARD OF NAPOLEON HILL!

I believe the happiest moment of my life was experienced a few weeks ago while I was making a small purchase in a store in Dallas, Texas. The young man who was waiting on me was a rather sociable, talkative, thinking type of young fellow. He told me all about what was going on in the store—a sort of "behind the curtains" visit, as it were—and wound up by telling me that his store manager had made all of his people very happy that day by promising them a Golden Rule Psychology Club and a subscription to one of my magazines, with the store's compliments. (No, he didn't know who I was.)

That interested me, naturally, so I asked him who this Napoleon Hill was, about whom he had been talking. He looked at me with a quizzical expression on his face and replied, "You mean to say you have never heard of Napoleon Hill?" I confessed that the name did sound rather familiar, but I asked the young man what it was that caused his store manager to give each of his employees a year's subscription to my magazine, and he said, "Because one month's issue of it has converted one of the grouchiest men we've got into one of the best fellows in this store, and my boss said if it would do that, he wanted all of us to read it."

It was not the appeal to my egotistical side that made me happy as I shook hands with the young man and told him who I was, but to that deeper emotional side which is always touched in every human being upon finding that his or her work is bringing happiness to others.

This is the sort of happiness that modifies the common human tendency toward selfishness, and aids evolution in its

work of separating the animal instincts from the human intu-
ition in human beings.

I have always argued that people should develop self-
confidence and that they should be a good self-advertisement.
I am going to prove that I practice what I preach on this subject by boldly asserting that if I had an audience as great as the
one served by *The Saturday Evening Post*—which I could serve
monthly through this, my little magazine—I could accomplish more inside of the next five years toward influencing the
masses to deal with each other on the Golden Rule basis, than
all the other newspapers and magazines combined have done
in the last ten years.

The upcoming December issue of *The Golden Rule* marks
the end of my first year, and I know it will not be construed as
an idle boast when I tell my readers that the seeds we have sown
through these pages during these twelve months are beginning
to sprout and grow throughout the United States, Canada,
and some foreign countries. Some of the greatest philosophers,
teachers, preachers, and businessmen of the age have not only
pledged us their hearty moral support, but they have actually
gone out and rounded up subscriptions for us in order to help
foster the spirit of goodwill that we are preaching.

MY TENDENCY TO NITPICK

Is it any wonder that your humble editor is happy?

There are people who have more, much more, of the worldly
wealth to show for their thirty-six years of experience than I
have, but I have no fear in challenging all of them to show a
greater stock of happiness than I enjoy as a result of my work.

Of course it may be only a meaningless circumstance, but to me it is quite significant that the greatest and deepest happiness I have experienced has come to me ever since I began publishing this magazine.

"What so ever a man soweth, that shall he also reap." Yes, it came from the Bible, and it is sound philosophy that always works. And my experience has proved conclusively that it does.

The first time the notion ever struck me to own and edit a magazine, some fifteen years ago, my idea was to jump on everything that was bad and pick to pieces all that I did not like. The gods of fate must have intervened to keep me from starting such an enterprise at that time, because everything that I have learned fully corroborates the philosophy in the above quotation.

HOW TO BE VERY HAPPY FOR THE HOLIDAYS!

Permit me to suggest a simple little service that you can render which ought to, and probably would, bring you great happiness and at the same time make others happy.

During the proper season, go out and buy some Holiday and New Year's cards.

Write some sentimental little messages on these cards, in your own handwriting, and then mail them—*not to your friends,* but to your enemies! Send a card to everyone you ever disliked and to everyone you believe ever disliked you. Make the message you write on each card suitable for the person you send it to.

It will not hurt you to try this. It may do you much good. One thing for sure, it will make you feel that you have been bigger, more broadminded and sympathetic this Holiday season than you ever were before.

These days, more than ever, concessions should be made by all of us. We have reasons aplenty for changing our attitude toward our fellows. This will make the world a better place to live in. You are not satisfied with yourself anyway, and that is a healthy condition, because no normal person is ever fully satisfied. You naturally want to make some change in your environment and in your habits for the future.

May it not be possible that you could do no better than to start now with a firm determination to cultivate tolerance, sympathy, forgiveness, and a sense of justice toward all your neighbors, those you do not like as well as those you love?

May it not be an excellent idea to begin now to cultivate the habit of self-reliance, good cheer, and thoughtfulness for others, knowing, as you surely will know if you stop to think, that these same qualities will reflect themselves in those with whom you come in contact, and that they will eventually echo back to you in greatly increased measure?

SEND SCROOGE PACKING

We have all been narrow-minded, selfish, and stingy in years gone by. We have fed our minds upon hatred, cynicism, and distrust. We have wished our neighbors ill; we have laughed when they were in trouble. Let us now forget these mistakes we have made in the past, and just once, if for no other reason than to experiment, rise above our former selves and be big-hearted and broad-minded!

You cannot fill your heart with love and hatred at the same time. These two human emotions make uncongenial companions. One or the other usually dominates. Which, may I ask, would you prefer to dominate in your heart? Which, do you suppose, would ultimately serve you best and raise you to the highest point of achievement?

By all means, buy those Holiday cards and try the experiment that I have recommended. It will bring a ray of sunshine into your life that will touch every atom of your being and cause it to radiate those qualities that prompt the world to call a person "great."

True greatness is first manifested in one's own heart! The world never discovers that greatness until the individual has discovered it. It may be a long while after you discover that you have risen above petty meanness, jealousy, hatred, and envy before the world discovers it, but one thing is for sure: This discovery will never be made by the world until it has been made by you!

When you begin to feel in the bottom of your heart that a great soul dwells within your body—that you have commenced the process of transformation from the old self to the new—it will not be long until others will make the same discovery.

You can take the first step in the direction of true greatness by sending out those Holiday cards to, all you have disliked and all you believe have disliked you. It will require effort on your part to do this. You will have to overcome that damnable quality of stubbornness, but you can do it, and it will be worth doing.

I do not know for sure, but I strongly believe that this experiment will be worth as much to you as anything that has ever happened in your life, provided that you are not one of those rare souls who have risen above those negative qualities that stand between most of us and the opportunity to enjoy happiness and the only real success that can come to any human being—namely, the chance to bring happiness to others.

The biggest truth I have discovered in all of my experience is that it pays—pays in both dollars and in sereneness of mind—to learn to forgive and forget the ingratitude and the unkindness of others. It is a wonderful thing to be able to feel and know down deep in your heart that you have risen above the common human trait of "striking back" and exacting your "pound of flesh" for every wrong done you.

Just how wonderful it is you can only know by trying it.

Then try it now!

In closing, I would leave with you this thought:

Who is there to stop you from thoroughly organizing yourself and climbing to the heights in any undertaking you may choose? Who is there with power enough to stop you, if you organized your faculties and directed your efforts to a definite end, in an organized manner? If you belong to that great mass called "wage-bound," who must be at a certain place at a certain hour every day of their lives in order to get the necessary food and clothing for existence, who is there to stop you from organizing your faculties to such an extent that you can eventually take a day off, at least?

Answer these questions! The answers may lead you out of the wilderness of poverty and failure into the light of success and plenty. Who knows without trying?

Printed in the USA
CPSIA information can be obtained
at www.ICGtesting.com
JSHW012028140824
68134JS00033B/2926